RENEWED

A Mind, Body, Spirit Approach to Self-Renewal

Katie LaPlant, MSW, LICSW

Edited by: Christian Scott

Renewed: A Mind, Body, Spirit Approach to Self-Renewal

Self-Published @ Createspace & Kindle Direct Publishing

©2016 by Katie LaPlant

ISBN-13: 978-1539392712

ISBN-10: 1539392716

Dedication

*This book is dedicated to my parents, **Robert Koerner and Patricia Koerner**. You are two of the hardest working and most dedicated people I know. Thank you for sacrificing so much for me. I am who I am because of you. I've learned what I've learned because of you. Thank you for always loving me, encouraging me and supporting me. Thank you for teaching me the skills you've taught me, educating me and most of all thank you for giving me my faith. Words will never express how much I love you and how grateful I am for both of you. While I know some of this book may be difficult for you to read, I hope you will be able to see the big picture and outcome which is how grateful I am for my life being exactly the way it is and everything you've done for me to make it that way. I love you with all of my heart.*

*This book is also dedicated to my 2016/2017 RENEWED group members, **Sherry, Michelle, Macie, Maggie & Claire; Natasha, Sarah, Ally, Sidney, & Liz; Meagan, Annie, Amanda & Heather.** Thank you for joining the RENEWED Program. Your participation and attendance helped me to write this book. It gave me an audience to write to and feedback to work with. It also gave me the validation to press forward with this book with each and every group we had together. Watching you all work through the ideas in this program has been an indescribable experience for me as a facilitator and writer. I am so honored to know each of you and so proud of all you've accomplished in group. I can't thank you enough.*

*Lastly, this book is dedicated to **Christian**. Thank you from the bottom of my heart for opening your heart to me through this book. Thank you for your openness, honesty, hard work and perseverance. I've enjoyed every minute of working with you through the RENEWED Program and look forward to watching your life and purposes unfold.*

Contents

Foreword

My Hope for You

My name is Katie LaPlant. I am a 37 year old wife and mother of three. I am also a licensed clinical social worker. I've been practicing in a clinical setting for about 14 years now. Within that time I've worked with so many people struggling with high stress, anxiety and depression, addictions, and other mental health issues. I've had great success working with people. Ages have ranged from 8 to 60 years old. I am happy to say that I've not only had great success helping people to understand and learn how to live a life of peace, but I've been able to help them do this naturally with minimal, or no medications. I believe that I've had this great success for one reason. That reason is because of my personal experience.

I begin this book by sharing with you my story. Childhood is where we learn rules, norms and expectations that shape our beliefs, thoughts, feelings, morals and values. Our childhood impacts what we believe in terms of who we are, how worthy we are, how we look, how we feel, who we become friends with and even who we date. It has an impact on what we do in our future. If you grow up in dysfunction, it will have a negative impact on all those things. And we all grow up in some kind of systemic dysfunction.

I am a survivor of anxiety and depression, among many other DSM diagnoses. You name it, I feel like I can relate to it. I've carried several DSM diagnoses throughout my life, both self-diagnosed and professionally diagnosed. I've met criteria for PTSD, Bulimia, Binge Eating Disorder, Social Phobia, Generalized Anxiety Disorder, Sensory Processing Disorder, Obsessive Compulsive Disorder (well, I'm still working on this one), and Depression. I believe there were times in my life where I've even met the criteria for several Personality Disorders. There are hundreds of diagnoses out there and I have both personal and professional experience with many of them.

I felt shameful about my struggles for many years. I spent years in therapy hiding who I am, medicating myself and feeling fearful that if someone found out, then they would think I am unworthy of counseling them. By opening up and sharing myself, I learned that the opposite is true. By opening up and sharing myself, I learned how to embrace my struggles and use them for good. I learned how to feel them. I learned how to love them. Okay, so now I'm getting a little carried away. I'm not really sure I love them, but I learned how to be grateful for them.

My hope in writing this book is that you will become educated about how stress impacts the nervous system. My hope is that by learning about stress, you will begin to understand your anxiety, depression, addictions, codependency, eating disorders, etc. My hope is that you will become aware of the things in your life that contribute to your stress. And lastly, my hope is that you will gain some perspective and insight that will allow you to make changes in your life to overcome these disorders.

This book is a guide with coaching questions at the end of each chapter to guide you through this journey. They are not meant to be your therapist. They are not meant to diagnose you. I use them to help my clients identify negative thinking, behaviors and patterns. The questions are meant to help you set intentions that will help you to let go of old ways and implement new ideas and new ways of thinking. You will need a journal and some quiet time to reflect on each chapter.

This journey is not an easy one. You can expect to encounter struggle before things get easier. This book is not a magic remedy that will "fix" you. It is work and it is hard work. It will challenge you to dig deep and look at your life through different eyes. My promise to you is this, if you give it a chance and do the work, then your life will change.

I highly recommend getting the support of an RCP Coach to assist you on this journey. An RCP Coach is a coach who has been trained to assist people through the RENEWED Program either privately or in a group setting If you are interested in this added support, please contact me by visiting my website at **www.mindbodyspiritcounseling.net** *or* **www.renewedmindbodyspirit@wordpress.com** *and I am happy to send you a list of RCP Coaches. Also, please check out RENEWED: A Daily Devotional for Self-Renewal on amazon.com that you can use while working through this book.*

Become a RENEWED Certified Program Coach!

If you are interested in obtaining the rights to use RENEWED in your practice with clients or for personal purposes of helping those in your social circle, please consider checking out my certification program at:
www.renewedmindbodyspirit.wordpress.com.

Prologue

My Story

"Do not let your past define who you are today, but allow it to help you to better understand who you want to be tomorrow."

Childhood

Like so many of you, my story starts at a young age. I was a very insecure and fearful little girl. I was raised in a home with my mother, father and two sisters. I was a middle child. My mother is a wonderful and caring woman who worked part-time as a registered nurse. She is an incredibly hard worker with a giant heart for people.

My father is a positive and happy man. He too is a very hard worker. My father became a successful business owner by taking a risk, leaving a job he was not happy in and opening a business of his own. He was rarely home, but when he was it was nice.

My parents were caring parents. They were very supportive of me and encouraged my education, my athletics, and me becoming an independent woman. They raised my sisters and me to become responsible young women, with a strong set of morals and values. Overall, they were very successful parents; the kind of success I hope to achieve as a parent one day. I had a good relationship with my mother growing up and she is my best friend today. I have a father who I admire and respect and am able to have great conversations with today. I am who I am because of my parents. I learned what I learned because of my parents and today my parents are two of my greatest supports and encouragement.

Another person who greatly impacted my childhood was my grandmother. She was 100% Greek, was loud and loved food. She died in her seventies and suffered many medical conditions including obesity. She triggered a lot of my anxiety growing up. She was very rigid with her thinking. She was emotionally abusive and sometimes even physically. Her expectations of children were completely irrational. She controlled my mother; therefore, she controlled me.

I was afraid of my grandmother. I grew up secretly in fear. I was too afraid to talk about it; therefore, I did not allow myself to feel it. I began to numb my feelings and blocked everything out mostly with food. I started having panic attacks and anxiety by age 7 or 8. I would lie in bed the night before having to see my grandmother and I would panic and cry. My feelings were never validated and I was not taught how to cope with them. I was just told to stop feeling it.

Looking back into my childhood I can see now that I struggled with so many things. I was a sensitive child who was *abnormally* uncomfortable in loud and busy environments. I can also see now that I was very intuitive. I could and still can sense feelings and emotions from peoples' faces, body language and energy; things that most people can't sense. This sensitivity contributed to me being anxious around people, places and things that were unknown. It also made it very hard to watch the way my mother was treated by my grandmother.

I learned at a young age to ignore my feelings. Like many of you, I learned to feel shame, guilt, fear and insecurity. I learned at a young age to become controlling to protect myself from being emotionally and physically hurt. I developed obsessive compulsive disorder (OCD) and social phobia by middle school. I will talk more about all of this in the next few chapters.

The interesting thing about my social phobia was that I was was extrovert with social phobia. I loved people and craved connection in relationships and fun, but inside I feared rejection and shame. I learned to use my extrovert personality to mask my anxiety. To this day people tell me they never would have guessed that I struggle with anxiety or social phobia.

By age 8 I began using food to mask and comfort my emotions. My eating disorder started out as overeating and comfort eating that quickly grew into binge eating. I was overweight by age 9 which impacted my body image and self-esteem. By age 11 I was dieting and restricting food and by age 15 using laxatives and diet pills. At age 19 my eating disorder turned into full blown bulimia where I binged on food and purged it with exercise, diet pills and vomiting. I hated how I looked and how I felt. Today I can see that my eating disorder was triggered by my OCD thinking. My OCD thinking was triggered by my social anxiety and generalized anxiety. It's no wonder I struggled in and out of depression my whole life. The anxiety was just too much to handle.

I struggled in school socially. I did not struggle to make friends, but I struggled to keep them. I had difficulty trusting people, so I talked about them. I feared rejection, so I stayed emotionally as far away from them as I could. I became so anxious around people that I sat far away from my friends in class. I was still able to mask my anxiety and nobody ever knew.

High School/College

My teen years and twenties were an absolute mess which is where some personality stuff comes in. I learned to behave a certain way to get my needs met. Sometimes this meant seeking attention from others by lying and manipulating or even dressing a certain way. Sometimes it meant making a bigger deal out of something than it really was to get attention. I did not do these things to hurt others; I did them because I was hurting.

I met my husband Steve in high school. We were 15 years old. I couldn't resist his cute smile and "Z. Cavaricci" pants. Plus he always had gum and bought me lots of food. I was a food addict so this worked very well for me. On a serious note, we fell in love freshman year of high school and spent the next four years together. Steve was and still is very good to me. I love him very much, but there was also a part of me that stayed in this relationship because it was comfortable. I feared men and talking to boys. My social anxiety kept me from being able to communicate with others. I hated myself and felt unworthy. I think part of me feared first dates and talking which made it very easy to stay in the relationship with Steve.

Steve and I parted ways our first year of college. That is when life really fell apart. I turned to partying, alcohol and sex to calm my social anxiety. I didn't know how I felt and I certainly didn't know how to deal with it. I just knew I didn't want to feel it anymore. Drinking alcohol allowed me to let loose. Unfortunately I can't say it allowed me to be myself because I was acting nothing like myself. Like food, I lost control when I drank alcohol. I did not know my limits and I drank way too much. I threw myself at whoever would give me attention. I was an active bulimic who hated herself. To this day I believe that I was in survival mode, desperately trying to make it in a world that I did not understand at all.

I got back together with Steve at age 20. I was in my third year of college at the University of New Hampshire. I was studying psychology. My goal was to become a clinical mental health counselor and own my own private practice one day. I was learning about addiction that year. That is when I realized I had a problem. I can remember it so vividly. I was taking a class on "Dysfunctional Family Therapy". We watched a movie about an alcoholic father and our teacher taught us about the *family systems theory*. He taught us about what it means to be dysfunctional; he taught us the roles and stages of change in a family system. As I read the course material and watched the movies he showed, my affect got flatter and flatter. My mood got more depressed and eventually my eyes were opened and my denial was lifted. At age 20, in the middle of my junior year of college, my life came crashing down.

I met with my professor briefly that year to ask some questions about what he was teaching. I rarely spoke to men unless I was drunk because they intimidated me. But I was desperate to learn more and he was the only person who was able to break through my thick denial. I remember telling him about the feelings I experienced growing up in my home. I told him about the roles that we were playing out in my family and how it all made sense after watching the movie he showed.

For the first time, I cried. And I don't mean I cried because I was hurt. I mean, I cried because I was devastated. I thought my family was perfect. That moment was the beginning of a long recovery. That moment was the beginning of the 15 years

of grief that I was about to endure. That moment was the beginning of my spiritual journey.

My eating disorder became extremely compulsive that year. I was obsessive about what I ate and compulsively purged it. I would workout with fevers and no sleep. I lost weight and was praised for it by family and friends. On the outside I looked like a new person, but on the inside I was dying. On the eve of my 21st birthday the best and worst thing happened. I binge drank that night. I drank shot after shot until I was so intoxicated that Steve had to call 911. I was nonresponsive to the world. After a terrifying ambulance ride to the hospital, I am grateful to say that I recovered; well, physically that is.

Four weeks later, I received a letter in the mail. It was my discharge summary. At the bottom was a recommendation for me to see a therapist. It made no sense to me at the time. I still didn't get the big picture. I needed help, but I could not see it.

I went to the University's Counseling Center. They immediately sent me outside of the school for help. At the time I did not understand why, but now I can see that the issues I was dealing with were not academic. They were personal and they were much more complex and serious than the school counselor could handle.

That spring I started therapy with my first therapist. Her name was Jodi. She was sweet, kind and gentle. So much came to light for me. By working with Jodi in therapy, I was able to gain insight on my issues of anxiety and began to learn about how it impacted my eating disorder. I also disclosed another dark secret that spring; it was the first time I talked about the impact of being molested by a family friend.

I went home that summer and binged, purged and exercised my way through it. With my education as a resource, little things began to make sense. *My family dysfunction* became clearer. Only this dysfunction did not only exist in my family, but it also existed in my relationship with Steve.

I started a Twelve Step program that year. And it was not because it was suggested by my therapist. It was actually an assignment I was given my junior year of college during a class I was taking called, "Alcoholism and Addictions". We were required to attend six AA (Alcoholics Anonymous) meetings to learn more about addiction.

I love telling the story about my first meeting. I will never forget it. I showed up with a bag of chocolate chips to listen to addicts talk about their addiction to alcohol. I laugh every time I think about it. In all seriousness, there was something I fell in love with during those meetings. There was a presence there that was unexplainable. It was something I felt deep within my heart. I had a lot of social anxiety, so talking with others out loud in a group was not my thing. But I continued to go back because of the strong presence and connection I felt in the room. It was that year that I learned about a Higher Power whom I choose to call God. It was that moment of my life that I began a spiritual journey and the Twelve Steps became the foundation of my faith. So I was now seeing a therapist and attending Twelve Step meetings thinking to myself, "Man oh man, I am messed up".

Marriage

I graduated in the year 2000 with a bachelor's degree in Psychology and moved back home. That summer was a nightmare. My weight reached the lowest I'd ever been. Clothes were falling off of me. I think my parents were worried and felt helpless because they did not understand my disorder. For so long I wanted to stand out, but I can clearly remember the anxiety I felt when my parents started confronting me about my weight loss. It all finally came out and I openly said the word eating disorder out loud to them. It was as if they didn't know I had one. They asked a few questions. You could see the anxiety in my mother. It radiated out of her. She immediately became defensive as if it was her fault that I developed an eating disorder.

That summer, questions were asked. I was grateful they were interested and happy they were trying to understand. But I felt like they did not like the answers I gave as to how I developed the eating disorder or why.

The energy in my house became unhealthy and I knew it. Intuitively I knew I needed to look for a "big girl" job so I could move out, so I applied for a counselor job at a psychiatric hospital on the children's floor. That fall I moved into a single bedroom apartment alone. It was the best two years I'd ever had!

I loved living on my own. Because of how my parent's raised me and the skills they taught me, I did well on my own. I worked full time and paid my bills. I loved working at the hospital with the kids. I was good at it and I felt like I was making a difference and giving back in some way. I learned so much during those two years.

Steve and I were engaged that year. He is an amazing man. He is kind and caring and would do absolutely anything to make me happy. Isn't that the perfect man? I thought it was, until slowly I began to learn that he had a binge drinking problem. I can remember cursing the classes I was taking at the time because I knew it was those classes that taught me this. I remember at one point swearing I didn't want to learn anymore because the more I learned; the more it tore my life apart.

But something inside of me pulled at me to keep going. I learned more and more about binge drinking and binge eating. Soon they became intertwined. They seemed so similar. I began to confront my husband about his drinking which caused problems in our relationship. I remember the day I told him that he needed to make a decision; binge drinking or me. It was devastating. I remember driving to a meeting that day sobbing and feeling completely hopeless and scared. Yet in the bottom of my chest; deep inside my heart, I knew that I was going to be okay and that I was doing the right thing.

What the heck was that feeling though? I had no idea. However, I knew it was comforting and bright; warm and good.

I finally got to the meeting where they were talking about codependency. I can remember thinking, "Are you kidding me?" So I did what I always did when I learned a new word. First I researched it online, and then I went to the book store. The bookstore is one of my favorite places. We have a love/ hate relationship. Education was the key to freedom, but it was also the key to my pain. The more I learned, the more I lost, or so I thought.

Learning about codependency changed my life. I began to learn that I cannot change or fix those around me; I can only change and fix myself. My relationship with my husband got much better once I stopped trying to control him. This change did not happen overnight. It took several years. But once again, there was a strong feeling in my heart that told me our relationship was worth it. So I listened to it once more and stayed in the relationship.

During this entire process I went through a period where I felt like I lost my family for a few years. I didn't physically lose them, but emotionally I felt detached from them. Today I work with a lot of young adults and have learned that detaching is part of the normal process of becoming an independent adult. I just did not know how to do it in a healthy way. There was a lot of pain that came up while processing my childhood. There was so much *anger* and *grief*. Unfortunately my parents were not able to understand my feelings or this process. I can actually remember my grandmother telling me to "Stop reading so much!" My grandmother was a religious person, but far from a spiritual person. She used the name of God and Jesus to punish and shame me. This did not help at all. It just made me feel scared, ashamed and guilty.

I married Steve in 2002. My parents were so supportive and helped us to have the most beautiful wedding. My relationship with my family got much better, but my eating disorder continued. It got really bad through my first few years of marriage. But let me tell you, I looked amazing! I was probably the most miserable I'd ever been. We went to Hawaii for our honeymoon and I can remember sitting down with the travel agent to book the trip. The entire trip we planned revolved around where I was going to eat and if the hotel had a gym. At this time in my life I developed full blown OCD (obsessive compulsive disorder) with food and my body. Meal times would cause panic and anxiety unless I had complete control over where we went and what we ate. I don't remember how long this part of my life lasted, but my husband will tell you it was the most miserable. He was a people pleaser and would never challenge me or tell me how he was feeling. He simply went along for the ride.

I started graduate school in 2002. Keeping up with my eating disorder was not as easy. I could not exercise as much as I wanted due to time constraints. Because I was married and had my husband's income, I was able to buy more of the foods I wanted. So overeating became easier. Also, there was more stress with trying to balance graduate work and my feelings of anxiety and depression. I became pregnant as planned with our first child in 2003. This was a very challenging and emotional time. I could not vomit, I could not use laxatives or diet pills and I was so big that over exercising was not an option. I was a mess.

Motherhood

I had my first son, Dylan in 2004. I began planning my diet for how I was going to lose the baby weight before he was even born. I did manage to lose most of the weight through Weight Watchers and exercise. But I can remember obsessing and feeling completely miserable through the whole thing; shaming and beating myself up for months and months. I really didn't know any other way. It was the way I treated myself since I was seven or eight. Dylan was born with some minor challenges. He had sensory integration challenges at an early age. He wanted to be held constantly. He struggled with keeping clothing on, loud noises stressed him out, and he began having fears, phobias and night terrors by 9 months old. His first word was "dirty". We thought it was cute at the time, but I knew "dirty" was not exactly a typical first word. That was the start of mothering a son with anxiety and OCD. But despite my education and personal experiences, I had no idea what was going on with him.

I got pregnant with my daughter, Hailey quickly after Dylan was born. She was rushed out of my arms at birth because she would randomly stop breathing. She was immediately taken that evening to Boston Children's Hospital where she lived for the first two weeks of her life. Those two weeks were a blur. I don't remember much about it except that I looked and felt like total crap. I also remember that food was still on my mind. My daughter was in the NICU at Boston Children's Hospital and I did not miss one meal. In fact, I loved being there because they had these amazing chocolate chip cookies that were the size of my head. I ate one every day. I began to love hospitals after that because of those cookies. Little did I know that I would be spending much more time in them with my third child.

Hailey came home after 2 weeks with a prescription of caffeine and a heart monitor. The monitor would go off if she stopped breathing. We were instructed to conduct CPR after calling 911 if the monitor went off. This definitely raised my anxiety levels to an all-time high. But I didn't really have a say in the situation. I was in complete survival mode, so I just went along with it and made sure to eat whenever I could to numb the feelings. For some reason that always helped.

Hailey slept in the bassinet beside my bed for three months. I was so exhausted one evening that I slept through the heart monitor alarm. My husband came running up more concerned about me because I did not wake up. And let me tell you that alarm is absolutely ear piercing. At three months old she was cleared of her sleep apnea.

We made it through the three months of Hailey's sleep apnea and one RSV pneumonia hospitalization. Still in survival mode, I continued to make it through each day using food as my comfort. Dropping the baby weight was much harder at this point and I never made it down to my pre-baby weight. I did however; find a way to continue to make my way to the gym each day because the pain and guilt of not exercising was just too much to bear.

I got pregnant with Tyler in 2006 and he was born in August 2007. All I can say is OH MY GOSH! I thought I had seen it all. I had a three year old who was afraid to get dirty, touch anything, sleep alone, be in public places and wanted nothing to do with boy toys which is another story for another day. I got through the three months of apnea and one pneumonia hospitalization with Hailey. But then, Tyler was born. All of my children have changed me in some way, but my experience with Tyler changed me the most.

Tyler cried the minute he came into the world and didn't stop for two years. He was my only child who had to sleep in the nursery at the hospital because I just couldn't do anything to make him comfortable. Tyler was a very sick little boy. He had trouble swallowing and breathing and would often times choke on his own saliva. He developed nine pneumonias in four years that we know of and was hospitalized twice. I can remember once again feeling that feeling in my heart and hearing that voice in my head that would say, "Something is wrong!" I will not go into detail, but I went through years of constant confusion and questioning.

I read so much information online about what he was experiencing, but could not find someone to listen to me and help him. His doctor made me feel crazy even though I knew I wasn't. I learned things about children no parent should have to learn unless they are a pediatrician or nurse. I can remember one time right before Tyler's second hospitalization that I was told not to bring him back to the doctor office until it had been three days. On the second day he passed out at home from coughing. He was running a high fever for seven days and was struggling to keep his eyes open. I called the office and told them that if they would not see him, then I would call 911. They told me to bring him in and we saw a different doctor who was so concerned that she rushed him over to the hospital where he laid for two more days with yet another pneumonia.

I fought the fear to people please and decided to fire his doctor and see the doctor who took care of him during this hospital stay. We have been with her ever since. She listened to me and referred Tyler to several specialists. Long story short, that voice inside my head was right. There was something very wrong. Tyler was diagnosed with a laryngeal cleft that caused him to aspirate liquids and food causing his recurrent pneumonias and illness. It was repaired and he is doing very well. Tyler was also diagnosed with other developmental issues such as verbal apraxia and sensory processing disorder. We were able to get him help for these issues and he is functioning quite well in 3rd grade.

Emotional Crisis

Throughout my childbearing years I worked as a clinical social worker in the Children's Department of a community mental health center. I was working toward my license part time. It was an amazing experience for me. I worked in community mental health for ten years. During those years I met a lot of clients. Some were as young as 5 and some were as old as 19. I could relate to their feelings of anxiety and depression. Because some of them were diagnosed with bipolar disorder, I decided to diagnose myself with bipolar disorder. I can remember sharing with two different therapists that I thought I had bipolar. I don't think they believed me.

A few years ago, during the time of Tyler's surgery, I decided to see a psychiatrist to get some psychotropic relief for the anxiety I was feeling. What I really wanted was a pill to stop my compulsive eating. At this point I had given up on ever reaching my pre-baby weight; I just wanted to stay in the overweight category of the BMI (Body Mass Index) scale. The psychiatrist diagnosed me with bipolar disorder and started me on minimal medications that had somewhat of a positive effect for a short period of time. After a few months the medications were increased by the psychiatrist and a year later I was being faced with a taking a second and third drug which was a pretty serious medication.

I was still overweight and completely obsessed with being a size 4 again. The medication wasn't doing a thing as far as I was concerned. If anything it was causing me to binge eat more. But the doctor insisted that I needed the medication. I told him "Thank you very much but I don't want it anymore." I asked for his blessing to help me to wean off the medication. He was very sweet and kind and agreed to help me, but did not agree with my decision. My therapist was worried too. I could see it in her face, but she whole heartedly supported me through the entire process and told me to go with my instinct that was screaming for me to get off these medications. Yes, it was that voice again.

I did wean off the medication. It was complete and utter hell. It took 3-4 months to regain balance in my body, mind and spirit. Once again, I cannot believe my husband stayed with me through it all. I was an absolute mess through the whole process. I had severe panic and anxiety accompanied by insomnia for three months. I almost caved in and took a medication for the insomnia, but fought through it. This period of my life made the most impact on me. Surrendering to that experience truly changed my life forever. During that time I questioned everything I learned about mental health, physical health and spiritual health. It was my moment of complete surrender.

Finding Balance

Through that experience I developed a relationship with my aunt who was learning how to be a yoga teacher. She taught me how to breathe and how to connect with my body. She also taught me some gentle yoga postures to help me relax. I could only do these things for about two minutes at first. My mind would race, my heart would pound and I needed to get up and move. I felt like I could not breathe.

That summer I met two holistic nurse practitioners. One introduced me to vitamins that helped with anxiety and sleep. The other helped me learn about how food affected my mental health. She encouraged me to try an elimination diet for a few weeks. I was so desperate to feel better that I did it. I cut every single processed food, dairy, sugar, caffeine and gluten out of my diet for four weeks. Then I slowly added foods back in. It was the start of learning how to listen to my body.

I could not believe how sensitive my body was as I added the foods back in. I got headaches from certain foods and I noticed body pains from others. I noticed gas, bloating and digestive issues. It was eye opening. I didn't stay on a clean diet for long because the desire to compulsively eat was stronger. Shortly after, I went back to my old ways of compulsive eating. I think I even purged a few times that year which was something I hadn't done since before I had children. But, I knew I was on the right path because I was sleeping better and feeling better.

That Fall I went on my first retreat to Kripalu Center for Yoga and Health in the Berkshires of Massachusetts. It was a terrifying, but life changing experience. I took a workshop on anxiety that weekend and learned about the inner critic voice in our heads. I began to implement what I learned into my life. Being at Kripalu healed my anxiety. Overcoming my fears and trying new things, talking in small groups with people I didn't know, crying in front of others, eating healthy food and practicing breathing and yoga techniques for the weekend all changed my life.

At Kripalu I learned how to take care of myself and more importantly why I need to take care of myself. I learned that weekend that I need to put myself first. So I began to do it. That year many things changed. I developed a very close relationship with God. My relationships with friends changed. I could not take care of my friends anymore because I did not have the physical or mental energy. I learned how to ask and accept help. I was not used to this and it was a challenge for me to accept help from others. But that voice and feeling in my heart told me that if I wanted to get better, then something needed to change.

Little by little my need to please others disappeared. Fear of people, criticism and judgment slowly faded. I opened a small private practice that grew quickly and left my job of almost 10 years. I lost friends in the process and fought with family that year, but I healed. All through this I continued to use food to cope with my feelings.

I recently decided to face the next challenge...my biggest challenge...my eating disorder. I call it my cross. My eating disorder has always been the cross I bear. I tried every diet out there. I tried Overeaters Anonymous and just recently was talked into trying a very expensive shake diet. I did lose weight for about 2 weeks, but gained 15 pounds back. I finally decided I needed to look at why I gained 15 pounds after all I had been through and all I had learned.

As my spiritual practices continued, the answers became clear as to why I was putting on the weight. About two years ago I lost a good friend. I considered her my best friend because she knew the deepest and darkest things about me. I shared my whole self with her. We shared our spiritual beliefs, our fears and our worries. She was my neighbor and dear friend. Our kids were friends and our husbands were friends. We vacationed together and even decided to do some spiritual healing work together. One day during her journey of growth she decided that she no longer wanted to be in a friendship with me. She refused to tell me why and abandoned the friendship without giving me a clear reason.

I tried several times to reach her, but failed. I spent two years of my life struggling with understanding why and how she could just get up and leave. I wondered why and how she could spend time with other women, but wanted nothing to do with me after all we had shared together. I questioned why I was so unlovable. I asked her for forgiveness; not understanding why I needed to be forgiven. I gave her the space she needed to figure things out.

I gained about 20 pounds while grieving the loss of our friendship. I became embarrassed and ashamed when I would run into her and drive by her house because it was noticeable that I was struggling with food by the amount of weight I gained. I wanted to hide. I knew it was time to go back to Kripalu for healing. I found a workshop by Geneen Roth on her latest book "Women, Food and God". I felt that intuitive feeling again, so I bought the book, read it and began the process of implementing her principles and guidelines into my life. But, I gained a few more pounds.

Something inside me pulled at me to not give up and keep learning and going. I knew I had no other choice. Every single attempt to lose weight failed. So I did. I attended her workshop which was the most amazing of them all. She taught us about intuitive eating which is the process of listening to our mind, body and spirit regarding eating. I continue today with the process of intuitive eating. What does it feel like eating? Am I mentally hungry or physically hungry? Recognizing when I am full has been the biggest challenge of all. The process of *intuitive eating* led to my lifestyle of *intuitive living*.

True Surrender

It has been about a year and a half since attending that workshop and starting an *intuitive living lifestyle*. So much has changed for me. What started out as learning how to listen to my body, turned into listening to my body, mind and spirit. They are all part of the whole. I wrote my first book after that workshop. It was intended as a coaching tool for clients to help them begin to dialogue and process their food journey. That book evolved into this program.

My spiritual life grew quickly after that workshop. I started doing things I would have never done before. Once I could feel what was going on inside me, I could begin to listen. Soon after I learned how to listen, I started to take risks and began obeying my intuition. I learned one very simple thing; if I take the risk and obey my intuition, then I will not fail. But if I ignore it; then I will become anxious, imbalanced and eventually depressed.

I still encounter daily challenges. I mean come on now, I am a wife and mother of three very busy children. All three children have their challenges. I am constantly battling the education system which can be very stressful. My kids are involved in karate, hockey and football which involve a very busy practice and game schedule. I have two puppies I am trying to train which has been very overwhelming. I am a small business owner and I am in the process of writing this program so I can share it with many others. And I am very involved in my church. Life still gets overwhelming, but today I know how to recognize when I am stressed and I know what to do to re-balance myself before it turns into a chronic anxiety or depression.

My hope in telling you my story is to help you to uncover yours. My guess is that you can relate to some of the feelings I felt and the experiences I went through. Please take a moment to reflect on my story. Take out your journal and write yours. What are some things you can relate to after reading my story? What are some of the challenges you faced growing up? How did they lead you to where you are now? What are some of the challenges you are facing now? And lastly, what do you hope to gain by reading this book?

This book will challenge you to uncover your story. It will teach you new ways to see your struggles and new ways to overcoming them. Today I live my life completely surrendered and most days I have a sense of peace and harmony even in the midst of complete chaos. And my mission is to teach you how to do the same.

Chapter One

Understanding Stress

"The first step toward making any kind of change is awareness."

Stress occurs every day, everywhere and in everyone. Stress affects a large percentage of the general population. People struggling with stress range from infants to the elderly in age.

The long-term impact that stress has on a person's nervous system is great. Often times stress will affect a person's mood and can even result in a clinical diagnosis of anxiety and/or depression. It can lead to people engaging in high risk or unhealthy behaviors to numb them and help them cope with feelings of fear, worry and insecurity. Lastly, stress can have a tremendous impact on relationships.

Last week I had a friend tell me that he doesn't know what is wrong with him. He said he simply feels exhausted and he doesn't know why. He told me that it's gotten so bad that he plans to see his doctor to discuss medication options. I looked at him with a flat affect, confused by how he really had no idea why he is so tired. He gets up at four AM to start his day and doesn't stop to rest until about eleven PM. He has a high stress job that is demanding, a busy family to take care of and recreational commitments to tend to. He does practice self-care by eating healthy, exercising regularly and feeding his spiritual needs through his church community and music, but he does not take enough time for rest. Instead, he tries to fit all the activities into his week and the result is fatigue and exhaustion. It has affected his mood, his behaviors and his relationships with family and friends. My friend expressed feelings, symptoms and long-term effects of stress which is the result of not listening to his mental, emotional, spiritual and physical needs.

A Psychological Explanation of Stress

The following explanation is my understanding of what happens to the body, mind and spirit when it experiences stress:

Stress is a chemical reaction caused by an increase in cortisol and adrenaline. When we experience a stressful situation or event, it causes sudden feelings of panic, fear or worry.

The feelings of panic, fear and worry make us uncomfortable, so our natural instinct is to respond by fighting back or trying to avoid the situation. Sometimes our natural instinct to these feelings is to freeze.

This kind of response does not solve anything. It simply makes it worse and over time the stress builds, sending more frequent and intense surges of adrenaline and cortisol throughout the body. If we experience stress on a regular basis, then our bodies adapt to the cortisol or adrenaline high and they eventually become unbalanced. If our bodies are unbalanced, then we can experience the rise in cortisol or adrenaline at any time, even when there is no external stressor. When this happens, it becomes difficult to rest, eat, exercise and do the natural things our body needs to rebalance itself and can result in a clinical diagnosis of anxiety.

Eventually the body becomes unstable which affects the balance of other chemicals such as dopamine and serotonin. When dopamine and serotonin become unbalanced, people can experience depression. This is the reason a doctor will prescribe a medication for a "chemical imbalance". Therefore, stress becomes a vicious cycle.

So, let's break this down:

1. **Stress is a chemical reaction in which we experience a rise in cortisol and adrenaline, in response to a person, place or thing that triggers feelings of fear, worry or panic.**

2. **Our instinctual response to the rise in cortisol is to *fight, flight or freeze*.**

3. ***Fight, flight or freeze* does not help. Instead it allows the feelings of panic, fear and worry to build, causing them to re-occur even if there is not an external trigger.**

4. **As the stress re-occurs and the brain becomes more unbalanced, the surge of cortisol becomes more frequent and intense.**

5. **Over time, as cortisol levels rise and become unstable, it affects the level of dopamine and serotonin usually resulting in some form of clinical anxiety and/or depression.**

Stress is just a feeling that causes a chemical reaction in the body. That's it! Our brains make it so much more. Our brains lie to us and tell us irrational things, creating a never-ending cycle of anxiety and depression. Medications can be prescribed and can work for many. However, in my experience, they cause multiple side affects and create instability of other hormones in the brain. This is why people end up on multiple medications for an initial chemical imbalance.

Stress on Mood, Food and Relationships

My guess is that you are reading this book because you are struggling with stress. Your stress may have led you to feeling anxious, depressed or both. It may have led you to engage in addictive behaviors such as drugs, alcohol, sex, shopping, or food. It may be affecting your relationships with family, friends or partners.

Over the last several years, I've worked with many teens who are struggling with high stress at school. We live in a culture where we push our kids from morning until evening. They don't eat properly, they don't drink enough water and they don't sleep enough. Electronics are taking over our world and children and teens sit in front of the screen instead of going outside to play. They sit all day at school and have test, after test, after test. They become overloaded with sensory and auditory information. The amount of stress and pressure they experience combined with the lack of nutrition, exercise and sleep has a serious impact on a child or teen's mood. After years of living with this kind of stress, they usually experience symptoms of anxiety accompanied by panic or sometimes even agoraphobia (fear of leaving the house). In time, the anxiety leads to depression.

Adults also struggle with high stress. Our culture does not encourage us to take time to unwind or destress. Instead, it pushes us to keep going, suck it up and fight through the stress. Half the time we don't even know we are stressed until it is too late. Like teens, adults do not eat regularly or nutritiously. They do not sleep enough hours and they do not get enough exercise. Many don't drink enough water and instead survive off of caffeine or energy drinks to stay awake and energized. Our culture has made it nearly impossible to recognize stress and anxiety because it's way of dealing with stress is to use some kind of quick fix or substance to numb and relieve it. Addictions have become high among teens and adults for this reason.

Relationships are deeply impacted as a result of the effects that stress has on our mind, body and spirit. Do you know anyone who is struggling with anxiety, depression, mood disorders, or addictions? If you answered yes, then please take a moment to reflect on how their disorders impact their lives, specifically with regard to their relationships. Take a moment to reflect on how their disorder impacts their relationship with you. Anxiety, depression and addiction are family disorders, not just individual ones.

It's been my experience that stress can and will build up over a period of time and cause an imbalance in my mood. I can become anxious for no reason at all, simply because the chemicals in my brain are imbalanced. If I am stressed, it affects my ability sleep. I toss and turn with racing thoughts and cannot seem to shut my brain off. When I am tired, I am less likely to cook healthy for myself, eat regularly, get to the gym or to my support groups that feed my soul. If I don't sleep properly, then I become irritable and sometimes even depressed, which affects my relationships.

At the beginning of this book, I shared with you my story. I shared my deepest and darkest secrets and all the things I grew up feeling ashamed of. I was not taught how to understand stress. I was not taught how to deal with stress because the people around me did not understand it. Instead, I learned to fear stress. I learned to avoid stress by using food to numb my feelings. The more I used food, the bigger I got. The bigger I got, the more anxious and depressed I became. Eventually my issues with food turned into bulimia as a means to control my weight and fit into the world I thought I was expected to fit into. I became depressed over time. My life became a life of chaos and stress instead of a life of peace and harmony.

In turn, I became angry, scared, lonely, and ashamed. These feelings led to feelings of insecurity, which affected my relationships with others. I never struggled to make friends, but I struggled to keep them. I was a negative person to be around. I found the bad in everything. I was irritable and controlling and never wanted to leave my house. I had little energy and was no fun to be around unless, of course, I was drinking or in control of what I was doing. And when things got hard in relationships, I ran from them to avoid rejection and pain.

How to Reduce and Eliminate Overall Stress

So in a nutshell, stress can lead to many different kinds of dysfunctions. In order to reduce or eliminate stress altogether, one must make the necessary lifestyle changes that will honor the mind, body and soul. These changes are based off of two very simple steps.

1. **Adopt an *Intuitive Living Lifestyle*.** This means learning how to listen to that inner voice inside of us that tells us what to do, when to do it and how to do it.

2. **Make self-care a priority by practicing *The Mind, Body, Spirit Approach to Living*.** By practicing self-care, we can eliminate unnecessary stress and maintain our intuitive connection.

Challenges You May Face

In order to make the changes I am guiding you to make, you will experience many challenges. As you continue through this guide, I will walk you through ways to adopt an *Intuitive Living Lifestyle* by practicing *The Mind, Body, Spirit Approach to Living*. I will also give you some examples of challenges you can expect to face in each chapter. The biggest challenge you can expect to face on this journey is grief. While change sounds nice, it is not an easy process.   Change requires us to adopt new ways of thinking and being and let go of old ways of thinking and being.

So Now What?

Now is the time to decide if you want to move forward with learning how to change your life and reduce overall stress. This is not an easy journey, but I can assure you that it is worth the effort you will put into making the necessary changes.

In the remaining chapters of this book I am going to teach you how to make those changes. I will use my experience both professionally and personally to teach you the things I implemented into my life to shift from patterns of self-harm to self-care and from a life of stress and chaos to a life of intuitive living; a life of peace and harmony.

Questions for Reflection

Find a quiet space where there are little to no distractions. Take a moment in quiet to reflect on what you just read. When you are ready, answer the following questions in your journal.

1. Does stress impact your mental focus? If so, then please explain.

2. Does stress impact you spiritually? If so, please explain.

3. How does your body physically respond to stress? Do you fight, flight or freeze in a stressful situation. Give an example.

4. Does stress affect you emotionally? If so, then please explain?

5. What people, places and situations trigger stress for you?

6. Do you engage in unhealthy behaviors to help you cope or numb stress? If so, then please explain.

7. Does stress impact your relationships? If so, then please explain.

8. Reread the definition I gave of stress. Reflect on it. Does understanding the physiological explanation of stress help you in any way? If so, then please explain.

9. What fears or worries do you have about adopting an intuitive living lifestyle and practicing self-care?

Chapter Two

Intuitive Living

"Intuitive living is learning how to live listening to that small voice in our soul that tells us what to do or how to do something, rather than listening to what our culture, society, family or religion tells us."

I grew up in an environment where I was not encouraged to listen to my body, mind or spirit. I was told what to do, what to wear, what to eat, how to look, how not to look, how to feel, how not to feel and the list goes on. My society, culture, family, and religion all played a part in that. Please do not misunderstand me. I value and appreciate my upbringing because there are many strengths and skills I gained from them. But for the purpose of this chapter, I am going to focus entirely on how those expectations kept me from being able to take care of myself, which hindered my growth physically, spiritually, emotionally and mentally.

I believe we are all born with an intuition. Some are born with stronger ones than others. But we are all capable of connecting to our intuition. I believe we learn at a very young age to ignore our intuition. Instead we learn to follow rules and expectations in our society. By neglecting our intuitive needs, we may suffer from high stress and adrenal fatigue, which leads to anxiety and depression. Our society pushes medication instead of spending the time and energy it takes to teach people how to take care of themselves. We live in a society that does not allow us to take time to nurture and care for ourselves. Instead, it shames us and makes us feel like we are selfish or lazy when we do attempt to take care of ourselves.

I can promise you that if you learn how to take care of your physical, emotional, mental and spiritual needs, then you will find yourself on less psychotropic medications. Some of you may even be able to eliminate medications all together. But before we can begin to practice self-care, we must first be able to connect intuitively to our body, mind and spirit, so we know when and how to take care of ourselves.

What is an intuition?

Every person has an intuition. It is a gift we are born with. It includes feelings and instincts, but more importantly a spiritual knowing or discernment. For example, I may be presented with a choice that includes taking a risk that I instinctually know is dangerous, but intuitively know will be okay.

Being intuitive is knowing something in your heart, in your mind and in your soul. When we connect to our intuition we can feel it emotionally, as well as sensually and spiritually. It is a knowing that we cannot describe or put into words.

Our intuition guides us spiritually, emotionally, mentally and physically. Our intuition is not God, but I do believe that God uses our intuition to communicate with us. Experts in neurology and psychology say that intuition is a sixth sense; it is a knowing based off of using the other 5 senses. So the more sensitive someone is, the stronger their intuition will be.

Highly Sensitive People vs. Empaths

Highly sensitive people are people who are unusually sensitive to sensory stimuli such as taste, touch, sight, sound and smell. Because of their heightened awareness, they tend to be extremely sensitive around people and new environments. They can appear anxious, uptight and on guard. They tend to detect danger faster than the average person because their senses are so sharp. Twenty percent of the general population is made up of highly sensitive people.

An empath is a highly sensitive person who is unusually sensitive to the energy and emotions of both themselves and others. They too have a keen sense of awareness with regard to taste, touch, sight, smell and sound. They can walk into a room and identify whether an environment is positive or negative. They tend to be gifted at reading people emotionally. They are a good judge of character by first impression. And they tend to take on the emotions and physical symptoms of those around them. Empaths can also appear anxious, uptight and on guard. Two to three percent of the general population are empaths.

Most of the people who come to see me for therapy are highly sensitive people. And some of those highly sensitive people are empaths. They go through life, struggling to manage their intense feelings and emotions. They usually end up anxious and depressed. They describe feeling different from others in their environment, especially those who are true empaths. But once they begin to understand their intuitive nature, they can begin to learn how to tap into their intuition and use that information to heal themselves, body, mind and soul. They learn to adopt a self-care practice that helps them to stay connected to their intuition and their emotions. They no longer live anxious and depressed.

What is Intuitive Living?

Let me ask you this. What would happen if you started listening to your intuition? Scary question, isn't it? The rest of this book will explore intuitive living. I will share my story of breaking free from social, cultural and religious rules and expectations that prevented me from listening to my intuition, as well as what happened when I started finally following my intuition. I will share with you, chapter by chapter, the steps you can take to start listening to your intuition to gain a happier, healthier and more peaceful life; a life free from the bonds of stress and anxiety.

I cannot promise that you will never feel stress or anxiety again because some stress and anxiety is normal. What I can promise you is that you will learn how to work through your stress and anxiety. I am NOT going to teach you how to make it go away. I am NOT going to teach you how to cope with it. I am NOT going to teach you how to manage it. I am going to teach you how to EMBRACE it and be with it until it is ready to leave. I am going to teach you how to be at peace with it and to be okay with it. And when you find peace with your stress and anxiety, it will no longer take over your life and bring you down; it will no longer consume you or hold you back. Lastly, I am going to teach you how to understand your stress and listen to what it is trying to tell you.

What Does it Take to Live Intuitively?

There were many things that needed to change in my life in order for me to begin living intuitively; the key words being, "needed to change". Most people do not like change. Change has a very bad reputation in our culture. We go to school so we can get an education and adopt the "50 year plan" as I call it. The "50 year plan" is the idea that you pick a career that you will do for the rest of your life. Our culture encourages us to pick a job and stick with it every day for the rest of our working careers, then retire and hopefully live a happy life.

My experience with the "50 Year Plan" is that it doesn't work for people. In my practice with clients, I see many who come to see me in the midst of a mid-life crisis, presenting with severe fatigue and anxiety. The outcome of our work together is usually a job change. They discover that the reason they are so miserable is because they never learned how to evolve and embrace change. I see teenagers who come to see me with severe anxiety, fatigue and depression because they are also stuck doing the same things every day and are not encouraged to explore their intuitive gifts or abilities. Instead, they are shamed for them. At such a young age we teach our children to stay stuck and to resist change. Why? Because let's face it, change is scary. But I learned the hard way, after a bout of severe anxiety and depression, that change is necessary if we want to evolve and grow as humans were created to.

So what does it take to evolve? The answer is very simple. It takes intuitive living. I've learned that our body, mind and spirit intuitively know exactly what they need and what they are supposed to do. All we have to do is take the time to listen and honor it. The following are a list of things I find are necessary if you want to adopt an intuitive living lifestyle.

1. **It takes desire and motivation.** The world we live in is hard. It can be extremely challenging and can feel like a lot of pressure sometimes. We are pressured to live like our family members and friends. We learn to ignore that voice in our heads because we fear what others will think of us or say to us if we go against the norm and listen to our intuition. In order to truly break free from this pressure, you must have the desire and motivation to push through some pretty difficult feelings and situations that will arise as you begin the process of change. If you are someone who is struggling with depression and have little motivation, that is okay. The motivation will come as you begin to work through this and see results.

2. **It takes discipline and effort.** Please don't shut the book just yet. I know these are some hard things to digest, but I want to be as real, open and honest as I can with you. My journey to freedom was not at all easy. I fought it many

times until I became desperate enough to surrender my way and to start listening to my mind, body and spirit. Once I started obeying the spirit inside of me, my world changed. My thoughts changed. My views changed. The people around me changed. But in order to get there, I had to make some changes in my life, which took discipline and effort. Self-care is a lot of work and it takes discipline and much effort to maintain a structured self-care program.

3. **It takes time.** Making changes is not easy for anyone. Over time we develop habits. Breaking habits and changing our ways can bring up feelings of fear and insecurity. Going back to the physiological explanation of stress, we know now that feelings of fear and insecurity will trigger stress which will be uncomfortable and make us want to fight, flight or freeze. It takes time to be able to recognize our behaviors and patterns that are getting in the way of listening to our intuition. Recovery and healing is a process and it takes time. I cannot wave a magic wand to make the feelings of fear and insecurity go away, nor will you learn how to live intuitively overnight. But with desire, motivation, discipline, and time, you will learn how to work through the feelings of fear and insecurity. You will learn how embrace them and find peace with them.

4. **It takes patience and persistence.** Yes people! I said the word patience. In our society, we are so used to immediate gratification. We are used to pressing a button and getting a result, reaction or an answer. My point is that we are not used to sitting still and waiting. People give up quickly if they don't see immediate results. This is a societal thing. And our society just keeps making us more and more impatient by creating new products that will gratify us quicker and quicker. If you really think about it, we don't have to wait too long for anything. People don't know how to wait. It makes them grumpy, uncomfortable and irritable to wait for things. We are always in a rush to get to the next

thing. And because of this, we give up quickly and give into temptations.

5. **It takes connecting to a Higher Power.** Okay, now you have permission to shut me out because yes we are going there. I am going to lay it out there and be one hundred percent honest with you right now. In order for me to truly heal from the stress, anxiety, depression and all of the other things I was battling, I had had to surrender to a spiritual power. Again, this power for me is God. I don't care what you choose to call God. I've worked with people who use the word Love instead. Whatever! I don't care. Use whatever you choose and whatever your intuition wants you to use. But just try to be open to connecting to this power because there is one. And if you just give me the time to tell my story, explain, and help you learn to connect to Him, then you will see what happens for yourself.

6. **It takes learning how to set healthy limits and boundaries.** Yikes! Did I just say boundaries? Yes, I did. Boundaries were very difficult for me to understand, learn and set with those around me. I am a people pleaser who knows how to give. I do not like to feel bad. Saying no to people made me feel bad. Standing up to someone made me feel mean. Taking care of myself made me feel selfish. And putting limits around my work, children, husband, friends, and family made the people around me very upset. When they were upset, I was upset. But learning how to set boundaries and be okay with boundaries is necessary if we want to have the time and energy to take care of ourselves and if we want to renew ourselves when feeling depleted.

7. **It takes building a healthy support system.** In order to make the necessary changes in your life I am teaching you about, we are going to talk about our support systems and how they aide in our recovery or how they deter us from moving forward. I am going to once again be one hundred percent honest here. It is likely that you will discover that

some of the people in your current support circle are actually toxic to your healing. It is likely that you will lose friends during this process and possibly even distance yourself from people you expected to be close with forever. We will talk more about this in chapters to come. In order to maintain intuitive living, one must have a healthy support system. This includes, but is not limited to the work environment.

8. **It takes self-compassion.** Now this is a hard one that we will spend a lot of time on. We are our own worst enemies. Many of us fall into that perfectionist personality where we give up because we feel like failures if we don't meet our own goals and expectations perfectly. In order to fully recover and live intuitively, you must learn how to be gentle with yourself and be self-compassionate.

Notice I said learn. Again, this is not something that will change overnight. You will slowly learn how to nurture and love yourself. But most of all, you will learn how to forgive yourself and let go of mistakes.

Challenges You May Face

During your journey, you can expect to go through many ups and downs and face many challenges along the way. I am going to give you a brief overview of the challenges you can expect to face as you begin this journey of intuitive living.

1. **You can expect to have changes in your social and/or work circle.** As I stated above, you will lose friends. Some friends will turn their backs on you completely and some will just distance themselves from you. You may also choose to leave certain relationships. Some people recognize that their work environment is toxic to their mind, body and spirt. Some find that their work environment hinders them from being able to maintain a more balanced self-care practice.

Either way, you can expect to encounter some losses along the way. But let me tell you this. I promise you that those losses will be replaced with better friends and a healthier work atmosphere; more supportive ones and ones that are healthier.

2. **You can expect the inner critic to rear its ugly voice.** We are going to spend a whole chapter on the inner critic. But for now just know that you can expect many visits from that negative voice in your head that tries to deter you from listening to your intuition; that voice that makes you feel scared and fearful of the unknown.

3. **You can expect to encounter grief.** This will be the hardest part of all. As stated above, you will make many changes in your life. For some, the changes affect your social circle. For some it is your job or career. For some it is your lifestyle. For some it is in your relationship with yourself. Anytime we go through a change in life, we need to accept the reality of the outcome we are about to endure. In order to reach acceptance, we must go through a series of stages called grief. These stages include denial, anger, shame and guilt, bargaining, depression and acceptance. In order to go through these changes, we must feel the feelings involved. This is not easy and certainly requires us to sit with feelings of discomfort. Most people get stuck in one of the above stages and never make it to the end stage of acceptance because they don't know how to embrace and sit through the feelings. Understanding grief and acceptance is vital in the recovery and healing process.

So Now What?

So now that I laid it all out there for you to read, I am hoping that you will continue on this journey with me. I promise you that it will be hard. And I promise you that things may get harder before they get easier. But I also promise you that the end result is far greater and much more powerful than what you will go through and it will be worth it. In order to begin healing your mood, behaviors, and/or relationships fully, you must begin to practice living intuitively. The next chapter will help you to explore how to begin and maintain that balance through self-care. All you need to do is continue the journey.

Questions for Reflection

Find a quiet space where there are little to no distractions. Take a moment in quiet to reflect on what you just read. When you are ready, answer the following questions in your journal.

1. Do you recognize your intuition? If so, what does it feel like? Describe.

2. What would happen if you started listening to your intuition? What things might be difficult and what things might change?

3. Looking back in this chapter at "What it Takes to Live Intuitively," what parts do you think might be challenging for you? Why?

4. Looking back in this chapter at "The Challenges You May Face," are there any that scare you? If so, then why? Please explain.

5. Describe your desire and motivation to learn how to live intuitively.

6. What do you expect to gain from learning how to honor your intuition?

7. What are some things you can begin to implement into your life in order to live a more intuitive living lifestyle? What needs to change in your life?

Chapter Three

From Medicinal Approach to Mind, Body, Spirit Approach

"In order to fully recover from stress and renew our mind, body and soul, we must find balance through the practice of self-care."

It has been my experience that many professionals treat stress solely from a medical approach. Many professionals have become rigid in how they understand anxiety, depression and mental illness as a whole and are often quick to prescribe a medication instead of spending the time it takes to talk with patients about intuitive living and self-care. Because of the changes in healthcare, providers are not given the time it takes to teach patients how to practice self-care. Often times providers do not ask questions that encourage their patients to connect intuitively and uncover what their mental, emotional, physical or spiritual needs are. In their defense, providers are trained to recognize and treat the symptoms.

This guide is going to help you to explore how a *Mind, Body, Spirit, Approach,* otherwise known as the practice of self-care, can help to balance our brain chemicals just as well as psychotropic medications. For many, you will be able to reduce the amount of medications you are taking and for some you will be able to eliminate medications all together. I am going to teach you how to honor what your body, mind and soul needs, rather than living to please those around you or rather than living making decisions based on what you think you are supposed to do.

The Medicinal Approach

Have you been to see a doctor lately? If so, please reflect on your experience for a moment. How long did your doctor spend with you? Did your doctor seem to listen to you and seem to understand what your concerns were? Did your doctor make any recommendations in the amount of time he or she spent with you? If so, what were they? Did your provider explain to you what he or she thinks is going on inside your mind and body based on his/her medical expertise? If so, what did he/she say? And lastly, did YOU have an opinion about what was being recommended and was YOUR opinion or input honored? I can answer all of these questions based off my experience with my doctors. I can also answer these questions based off my experience working with the doctors of my clients.

In my experience both personally and professionally, most doctors spend about 30 minutes with their patients during an annual visit. If you are someone on medications and are seeing a doctor for medication monitoring, the time they spend with you is about 15 minutes. They ask a few questions, make an educated guess as to what is going on based off their experience and education. They make a few recommendations, which are usually some kind of medication or quick fix, then send you on your way. Often times they do not ask the patient what they think is going on. Often times they do not educate the patient on what they are experiencing. Often times they do not try natural medicine. Instead, they leave their patients feeling uneducated and powerless.

I had a client I was working with named Michelle. When Michelle came to see me, she was experiencing tremendous anxiety and depression, accompanied by suicidal thoughts. Her doctor started her on medication and recommended psychotherapy. After working with Michelle for just a short period of time, she was able to identify where her anxiety was coming from. She discovered that she had an underlying diagnosis of PTSD that was constantly being triggered by her environment, which released a hormone called cortisol as learned about in chapter one. The constant ups and downs created adrenal fatigue which lead to insomnia, panic and eventually depression.

Michelle took some time off from work and began to re-learn how to take care of herself. This included adopting a self-care plan that nurtured her physical, emotional, mental and spiritual needs. It included eating regularly throughout the day, drinking more water, engaging in mild to moderate exercise, taking vitamins, journaling, praying, meditating, attending support groups, taking mental breaks during the day, going to church, and attending therapy on a regular and consistent basis. These activities became Michelle's medicine which replaced her psychotropic medications. Her panic, insomnia and anxiety decreased and her suicidal thinking was gone.

When she started to feel better, Michelle went back to work slowly. At first she was okay because she was working minimal hours that allowed for her to continue to nurture herself the way she needed to in order to maintain balance. Unfortunately, her position at work was a demanding, full-time position, so she was expected to either go back full-time or lose her job. She went back full-time. She ended up back on all medications and in an outpatient treatment facility.

I can remember talking with her doctor to coordinate care. I explained to Michelle's doctor that Michelle was fatigued from years and years of stress. I encouraged her doctor to treat her adrenal fatigue rather than her mental health. Her doctor did not listen to anything I had to say regarding Michelle's mental health. She did, however, agree that Michelle would benefit from a lifestyle change. But I felt like she viewed Michelle as weak and mentally ill, while I viewed Michelle as being resilient, strong and brave. Changing a lifestyle is extremely challenging and takes a tremendous amount of work and dedication. It is scary to give up jobs that provide financial stability and comfort. It is scary to go against our doctors' recommendations and it is scary to make the decision to take care of ourselves without the support and understanding of those around us.

After Michelle completed the outpatient program, she decided to leave her full-time corporate life and work part-time in a less demanding environment where she had more flexibility and much more support. She did this so she could continue with her self-care plan which included having time to prepare and eat healthy meals, exercise regularly, attend groups and classes that met her mental and spiritual needs, go out with friends, and be able to spend time with her grandson. I am happy to say that today she is working part-time, taking care of her grandson who has severe medical issues and I just learned last week that Michelle is completely medication free. She will be the first to tell you that life is not perfect, but it is good.

I love Michelle's story and think the world of her. I've been blessed by her in so many ways. Her story is my story. Her story, also, may be some of your story.

The Mind, Body, Spirit Approach to Living

The *Mind, Body, Spirit Approach* to living is learning how to connect to our intuition and fulfill our physical, spiritual, mental and emotional needs, regardless of what our society, culture, family or religion says. It is learning how to renew ourselves through practicing physical, emotional, mental and spiritual self-care and living intuitively to maintain that balance.

PHYSICAL SELF-CARE
Our physical self-care is how we take care of our physical

body. The following is a list of physical self-care strategies:

- Eat healthy, whole, unprocessed foods regularly throughout the day to fuel your body giving it the energy it needs and to maintain adequate blood sugar.
- Drink 8-10 glasses of water a day to flush out toxins and stay hydrated.
- Engage in movement daily to stimulate endorphins and to flush out toxins from the body. Movement can include housework, yard work, traditional exercise such as lifting weights or running on a treadmill, swimming, hiking, dancing, etc.
- Get 8 hours of sleep a night.
- Get to the doctors.
- Take vitamins to supplement deficiencies and aid in proper nutrition and digestion.

EMOTIONAL SELF-CARE
Our emotional self-care is how we feed and nurture our thoughts and feelings. The following is a list of emotional self-care strategies:

- Conquer the inner critic and let go of perfectionism.
- Practice gratitude every day by being mindful of the things that are going well in your life rather focusing on the things that are going wrong.
- Set healthy limits and boundaries by learning how to say no.
- Learn how to ask for help and receive it.
- Build a healthy support system.
- Learn how to grieve.

MENTAL SELF-CARE
Our mental self-care is how we stimulate our brains intellectually. The following is a list of mental self-care strategies:

- Read a new book that fosters growth.

- Take a class or attend an upcoming workshop in a topic of interest to you.
- Sign up for a new blog.
- Attend an online seminar or telecast by phone.
- Start blogging or journaling.
- Take a vacation to reset from your everyday, busy life.
- Abstain from social media for a period of time.
- Do an activity that elicits laughter, as laughter is scientifically proven to change the chemicals in the brain.

SPIRITUAL SELF-CARE
Spiritual self-care is how we nurture and connect spiritually to foster growth and live out our purpose. The following is a list of spiritual self-care strategies:

- Explore your spiritual beliefs.
- Get connected spiritually through music, writing, nature, prayer, meditation, yoga or other movement.
- Express yourself creatively through music, drawing, writing, painting, acting or sewing.
- Adopt an intuitive living lifestyle to help you meet your needs, balance your mind, body and spirit and discover your purpose.
- Surrender to God.
- Take risks and live out your bucket list.

How to Practice The Mind, Body, Spirit Approach to Living

Understanding the *Mind, Body, Spirit Approach to Living* is much simpler than practicing it. In order to fully embrace the Mind, Body, Spirit Approach to Living, one must make self-care a priority.

1. **Decide what areas of self-care you need to make a priority in your life.**

2. Decide what needs to change in order to make self-care a priority in your life.

3. Decide how you need to change these things.

Whatever changes you will make, I assure you they will be worth it, but you must make the commitment and decision to do it.

Challenges You May Face

The biggest challenges most people face when making the decision to adopt a self-care practice is time and effort.

TIME
Self-care is not a quick fix. It takes time to do the things we need to do to take care of ourselves naturally. This may mean changing our priorities. It may mean cutting our hours at work. It may mean letting go of mindless activities to make room for self-care. Most importantly, it may mean letting go of our expectations of self and others in order to make time for self-care.

EFFORT
It takes energy and effort to make any kind of change. It takes effort to push through the feelings we are going to encounter and losses we will face while making the necessary changes we will make. It takes effort to push through the resistance we will face from others as we begin to make the necessary changes we need to make.

So Now What?

In order to fully recover from stress and renew our mind, body and soul, self-care must become a priority in our lives.

Accepting this challenge and making self-care a priority is the hardest part of this journey. As I stated in the beginning pages of this book, recovery is a lot of work and it takes time to change habits and behaviors that will re-wire our thought patterns.

Take some time to assess your desire and motivation for making the self-care a priority. Be honest with yourself with where you are at in this journey. Practice self-compassion by allowing yourself to be exactly where you are in this journey without projecting shame or judgment onto yourself. And know that if you choose to stop now, that you can return to this book when you are ready.

Questions for Reflection

Find a quiet space where there are little to no distractions. Take a moment in quiet to reflect on what you just read. When you are ready, answer the following questions in your journal.

1. What has your experience with doctors been? Please describe.

2. Do your medical experiences impact how you view self-care? Please explain.

3. Do you currently have a self-care practice? If so, what does it look like?

4. What areas of self-care do you need to make a priority?

5. What strategies listed in this chapter can you implement into your lifestyle to take better care of yourself? Are there any strategies that were not listed that need to become part of your self-care practice?

6. After reading this chapter, write your short-term goals for implementing self-care into your life.

7. After reading this chapter, write your long-term goals for implementing self-care into your life.

8. What are some challenges you expect to face as you begin to set goals and make self-care a priority in your life?

9. What steps can you take today to begin making your self-care a priority?

Chapter Four

Understanding Rules and Expectations

"Rules and expectations keep us trapped in our heads, but acceptance frees us from bondage to self and others and allows us to see the world anew."

We are now heading into the meat of our healing process. First we've established our goal for reading this guide, which is to learn how to reach a balanced state of mind, body, spirit through intuitive living. Second is to maintain it by practicing physical, mental, emotional and spiritual self-care. In this chapter, we are going to explore the societal, cultural and religious norms and expectations that keep us stuck and hinder us from practicing intuitive living and self-care. We will explore ways to begin to let go of these expectations and rewire our thinking. And lastly, we will talk about the challenges you can expect to face as you begin to rewire your thinking and let go of unhealthy expectations of yourself and others.

The RENEWED Program consists of three areas of self-renewal: Mind, Body, and Spirit. Mind will include a person's emotional and mental well-being as it relates to themselves and others. It will also include intellectual and mental focus. Body will include a person's physical well-being as it relates to sleep, exercise and nutrition. Spirit will include a person's relationship with self, others, art, music, literature, nature, or a power greater than oneself. Throughout this book I will use my personal and professional experiences to explain how societal, cultural, religious and family rules and expectations impact the mind, body and spirit.

Expectations that Affect the Mind

We are born with the ability to feel human emotion. Let's face it, feeling emotions can be challenging. Positive emotions feel good, but negative emotions feel bad. As I said earlier, when we feel negative emotions, our bodies go into *fight, flight* or *freeze* mode. As a result, people have learned over time to avoid or fight negative emotions. In our society, feeling has become unacceptable unless it is something that feels good. We raise our children to grow up in homes where they are not allowed to cry and instead are punished or shamed for it. They are called "babies" or "immature" if they express stress and emotion. Teenagers are told they aren't going to make it in the real world when they express stress or anxiety. We raise daughters to learn that they are "too sensitive" if they express emotions and our boys to learn that they are "mama's boys" or "gay" if they express emotions. But in reality, emotions are natural and healthy.

Our family rules and norms have a tremendous impact on what we expect of ourselves and others with regard to emotional and mental well-being. I grew up in an environment where I wasn't allowed or encouraged to feel my feelings. Instead I was judged, shamed, scolded or criticized. I felt deeply misunderstood by those around me. I was a very sensitive child who could feel emotional energy that the majority of people could not feel. I could walk into a room and feel overwhelmed by the amount of energy or type of energy in a room. If it was too noisy or chaotic, I would flee or shut down. If someone was angry, I could feel it and I would shut down. My feelings were not honored because most of the time they were not understood.

Children need to be taught how to do deal with emotions. Managing emotions comes with maturity through learning how to relate with others. I grew up feeling very insecure with myself and the environment I lived in. I never felt safe and didn't trust anyone with my feelings because my feelings were always judged, shamed or minimized.

Society has unrealistic expectations of humans. Our American culture expects people to push their bodies and minds without ever allowing them to feel the human emotions associated with stress and anxiety. We are expected to grieve loss and changes without ever feeling any of the feelings that help us transition through the loss or change. And because it is unacceptable to feel, we are not taught how to deal with the emotions.

Feelings and emotions are normal. We were born with a brain that feels emotions for a reason. Our emotions and feelings tell us when something is wrong, but we don't always listen. Because we do not listen to these feelings, we live in a culture with a rise in people who are on psychotropic medications for anxiety and depression. Again, the message is, take a medication because it's not normal to feel.

Today I find that when I allow myself to feel and I honor these feelings, then I am able to let them go. Pretending they are not there, avoiding and pushing them out, and fighting them only keeps them stuck. Feeling our feelings is a good thing. Feeling scared means we need to be careful of something or it means something is not right. Feeling stressed means we need to take a look at how much we are doing and reassess our limitations. Feeling happy means something is good. Feeling angry means something is wrong. Feelings are internal cues that communicate to us when something needs to change. But our society does not like change. In fact, our society does everything in its power to stop change.

I always tell my clients that life is meant to evolve over time. Unfortunately, we live in a society where we are expected to grow up, go to school and after school get a job that we will have for the rest of our lives, or at least until retirement. For some people, this may work. But for the majority, they end up miserable at age forty-five because they never allowed their lives to evolve. They are not allowed to feel or express their misery and instead, their doctors prescribe them a pill so they can continue to do their job, which is the exact thing that is making them miserable.

I don't think there is anything wrong with going to school and planning for a specific field of expertise. However, I have learned that we grow mentally, emotionally and spiritually over time. Our passions grow and our jobs sometimes grow.

I worked in community mental health for 10 years. As life went on, I grew emotionally, mentally and spiritually. As a result, I evolved and am now on my own, working in private practice and writing. I couldn't be more fulfilled. Was I content in community mental health? Absolutely! But my passions grew and evolved into a spiritual passion. Community mental health was holding me back from being able to express that. So I had to change environments and jobs. But like I said, I took a risk and couldn't be happier.

Life is meant to evolve. Relationships are meant to evolve. Our society does not encourage these changes and instead creates rules where people learn that it is weak to feel emotions; it is bad to change who you are or where you work. Our society keeps people stuck.

Expectations that Affect the Body

I grew up in a home and culture with many rigid rules around the way my physical appearance should look in order to be considered beautiful. There were also rules with how I should and should not take care of my body. As discussed above, care of the body includes sleep, nutrition and exercise. My culture did not teach me how to be intuitive with my body. Instead, it taught me rules regarding how it was supposed to look. These rules still exist today and don't take into consideration that people come in all different shapes and sizes. Different people have different needs.

We have the BMI which tells us how much we should weigh on a scale based on our height and age. We have nutritionists who tell us how many calories we need to consume each day to be considered healthy or to maintain a healthy weight for our age. We have doctors who reinforce this. We have television and other media that reinforce what our bodies should or should not look like. People who are "overweight" according to our culture are called "fat" on t.v.

Have you seen Pitch Perfect the movie? It's a very funny movie, however, one of the girls in the movie goes by the name of "Fat Amy". She tells her peers that her real name is Patricia, but she goes by "Fat Amy" because she is considered "Fat" in the American Culture.

I grew up in a home with a lot of rules around what my body should look like, how much I should weigh, when I should eat, how much I should eat, what times I should eat...you get the point. Rules, rules and more rules. Because of these rules and expectations, once again, it kept me from learning how to listen to my intuition and honor myself.

Today we have a rise in eating disorders because our society sells us large quantities of high calorie and high fat processed foods that our bodies cannot handle, yet expects us to look like super models. It is absolutely absurd. In order to look the way our culture expects (which is unnatural to begin with), people have developed restrictive eating patterns otherwise known as diets or we purge through diet pills, exercise or vomiting.

Our culture tells us that we should be eating three meals a day with snacks in between, but our society doesn't give us the time to be able to sit and eat our meals. Do you know anyone who actually takes a lunch break at work? And think about our children's lunch at school. They are given 20 minutes for lunch. In this time, they are expected to transition to the cafeteria, go through the lunch line, sit and eat their lunch. And they are expected to do it all in 20 minutes.

We are expected to rush through our meals which is bad for our digestive systems. We are not given time to nourish our bodies the way they were created to be nourished, nor does our society encourage the foods and things our bodies need.

When humans first existed their bodies were created to work for food. They did not have cars to drive them to get their food. They hunted in forests for food and walked on foot. They built shelter with their hands. They did not have cell phones to talk to their friends. They had to walk to see them and they played creative games outside. Kids do not play outside anymore. They do not play creatively anymore. Electronics have taken over. Bottom line is that we do not move enough today. Many of us have jobs where we sit all day, cars we drive in and it is even worse today because socializing doesn't require any physical effort due to the growing technology. We are lacking in movement. Our doctors and nutritionists recommend exercise, but who has time to exercise when our culture is to work 10-12 hour days and then go home eat dinner and do homework or take our kids to their after school events.

And don't even get me started with sleep. Our bodies and minds were created to wake up when the sun rises and go to bed when the sun goes down.   Humans got more sleep in the winter and less in the summer. Our society does not at all live this way. People have jobs all hours of the day. Most people who come to see me tell me they are getting 5-6 hours of sleep a night. And that is on a good night. We are expected to be up early to get ready for work or school, yet we go to bed late at night in order to finish everything we need to get done in a day or watch our favorite television show that is on at 10pm.

Expectations that Affect the Spirit

Spiritual rules consist of rules that affect how we relate to ourselves, others, music, literature, nature, art and/or a Power Greater than us. I don't know about you, but I remember lots of rules growing up with regard to my spiritual beliefs. Infact, I don't even think I can say my beliefs were my beliefs because they were taught to me. My beliefs were based on religious beliefs.

I grew up in the Catholic Church. The Catholic Church taught me that in order to be a "good" Catholic I had to go to church on Sundays. Another rule to be considered "good" was that I had to fulfill the sacraments and traditions in the church. In order to marry in a church you have to complete a first penance, first communion and confirmation. Otherwise, you are not considered a Catholic and cannot get married in a church.

There are so many traditions and rules I appreciate now that I am adult, but they do not determine whether I am a good person or not. Let me tell you why. I spent my whole childhood in a Catholic church with a priest who preached all these rules about how we "should" live to be considered worthy or God's love for us or not. One week before I got married, this same priest was arrested and put in jail for molesting young boys. Practicing rules and traditions does not make you a good person. Practicing rules and traditions does not mean you are worthy of God's love for you. God loves us no matter what. God's love is unconditional. Those beliefs are not taught in many churches because the rules and traditions contradict this and create judgement and barriers. The rules create shame and guilt. God's plan for us is to feel loved, not guilty all the time.

Another harsh rule I grew up with is that God is a God that punishes if you do something bad or break the commandments. I do believe in commandments today, but I also know that we are human and we mess up a lot. But today I know that God is a loving God who does not punish, but forgives.

Making the decision to leave my religious denomination was very difficult. My family's beliefs and traditions shaped my life and it was hard going against the family norms and being different.

Some people have a difficult time with the idea of God. If you are one of those people I encourage you to explore why you struggle with this. What do you know about God? What were you taught and how did that impact your belief system today?

Some of you will answer these questions and still have trouble believing in the existence of a Higher Power. The purpose of this book is certainly not to try to persuade or convince you to believe in God. The purpose is to help you to believe in something. So the questions in this chapter will help you to explore just that. And it is okay if you do not believe in the traditional God. But I highly encourage you to explore your beliefs and think about why we are here on this earth. How did we get here and what is our purpose as humans?

I think our culture does not allow us to explore our faith anymore. Unfortunately people get offended easily and feel that it is their duty to defend their beliefs instead of listening and trying to understand someone else's. Quite honestly, I don't think any of us have all the answers. Nor do I think we will until the end of our life here on earth. What I do know is that too many things are too coincidental and the only explanation to some of those things is that they will never make sense because they are not supposed to and because our human minds are not meant to understand them. And as I study intuitive living and practice self-care, I am learning that **we all have similar beliefs, we simply use different words and phrases to describe those beliefs. We have religious**

rules that keep us separated and tell us that it is not okay to believe in an idea because it does not coincide with our religious beliefs.

I am very secure in my faith. I know what I believe and I am not afraid to keep an open mind and learn about new age thoughts and ideas, nor am I afraid to explore the old traditional ideas. The more I listen and learn, the more I grow. No matter what I come across in terms of information, I always bring it to God and ask Him what He wants me to see in it. My *relationship* with God is the basis of my faith. The words I use, the rules or traditions I believe in and follow and the information I choose to study doesn't matter unless I bring them to God and ask Him what He wants me to do with them.

How to Let Go of Rules and Expectations

The rules and expectations we learn to have with ourselves and others greatly impact how we view the world we live in. Those rules and expectations create the negative stories we tell ourselves in our minds, otherwise known as the inner critic. In order to fully recover from stress, we must re-create these stories in our minds. We do this by letting go of the learned rules and expectations we have of ourselves and others. The following are the steps we need to take to begin letting go of the rules and expectations we have.

1. **Explore and identify the rules and expectations you have of yourself and others with regard to mind, body and spirit.**

2. **Learn to identify your inner critic with regard to these rules and expectations you've learned.**

3. **Learn to grieve in order to fully let go.**

4. **Practice acceptance through prayer.**

5. Surround yourself with like-minded people who are also on a spiritual journey like you.

6. Practice self-compassion by allowing yourself to "just be" without criticism, judgement and shame.

Challenges You May Face

1. **Your inner critic will become stronger before it becomes weaker.** As you begin to think differently, your inner critic will challenge you by creating negative stories in your mind about how what you are learning and doing is "stupid and won't work." I find that the inner critic gets stronger as a last effort to hold you captive to your negative thoughts.

2. **It takes time and patience to learn the things you are about to learn.** Because our society is used to quick fixes, you will find yourself impatient and wanting the changes to happen over night. Rest assured knowing that this is a journey and it takes time and patience to change thought patterns that you've had most of your life.

3. **You can expect to feel alone at times and like the people around you do not understand.** As I began understanding how rules and expectations in my life impacted my ability to take care of myself, I started to make the necessary changes in my life to conquer the inner critic and practice self-care and self-compassion. Many people in my life did not understand the choices I was making and some even were upset and disappointed with me. You see, when we change, it forces the people around us to reflect on their choices. When they reflect, they are faced with a decision to then make changes in their lives. This can be very scary for the people around us. Sometimes their reactions will be positive. But often time, their reactions will be to flee from

you and you can expect to feel lonely at times.

So Now What?

Don't you see? Our culture has made it nearly impossible to take care of our physical, emotional, mental and spiritual needs. We just keep pushing ourselves and expecting more. We live by rules and expectations that are unrealistic and irrational. And because we have these unrealistic and irrational expectations of ourselves, we in turn have them in our relationships. It is a never ending cycle of abuse. It's no wonder people are struggling with mood disorders, addictions and relationship failures. We are never good enough. Our families are never good enough. Our children are never good enough. Our relationships are never good enough.

Take some time to reflect on the cultural and family rules, expectations and norms that have impacted your ability to take care of your whole self. In order to do that, you must first reflect on what your needs and beliefs are. Practice self-compassion by allowing yourself permission to explore these areas without criticism, judgement or shame.

Questions for Reflection

Find a quiet space where there are little to no distractions. Take a moment in quiet to reflect on what you just read. When you are ready, answer the following questions in your journal.

1. What are the rules, norms and expectations in your society/culture/family and religion that impact your ability to take care of your emotional and mental needs? How do they impact you?

2. What are the rules, norms and expectations in your society/culture/family and religion that impact your ability to take care of your physical needs? How do they impact you?

3. What are the rules, norms and expectations in your society/culture/family and religion that impact your ability to take care of your spiritual needs? How do they impact you?

4. How does understanding the rules, norms, and expectations in your society, culture, family, and religion help you to move forward in your intuitive living journey? Does it change the way you think or view your current situation or beliefs? If so, then how? Please be specific.

5. How can you begin to let go of the rules and expectations you have of yourself and others that are not benefiting your mind, body, and soul?

6. What are three ways you can practice self-compassion during this process?

Chapter 5

Conquering the Inner Critic and Letting Go of Perfectionism

"We are perfectly imperfect people and we do perfectly imperfect things. Humans makes mistakes. If we were perfect, then we would not be human."

What is *the inner critic*? The answer is simple. It is that internal voice in your head that is constantly criticizing and judging you. It is that voice in your head that is telling you that you are too fat or too thin. It is that voice in your head that is telling you that you are not good enough. It is that voice in your head that tells you that you are wrong or that you are stupid. You get the point. We all have an inner critic. But where does that voice come from and how do we overcome it?

Understanding the Inner Critic's Motives

I mentioned earlier that a couple of years ago I went on my first ever retreat to Kripalu Center for Yoga and Health. On that retreat I attended a workshop on Calming the Inner Critic. I learned so much about myself at this retreat. I also learned how to minimize my inner critic and to begin building up my inner coach. I want to share with you some things I learned about the inner critic and how I began to implement this new perspective into my life to help me to overcome my anxiety and depression.

If you are anything like me, your inner critic is very intense. For years my inner critic controlled me. It told me that I had to do things that did not fulfill me or make me happy. It told me that I had to do things in order to be accepted and liked. It told me I had to look a certain way in order to be loved. It kept me from achieving goals and it kept me from living life. It also kept me from living my life with purpose.

Inner critics develop early in childhood. Children want more than anything to be loved and accepted by their parents. Children are loyal to their parents whether they are being taught good things or bad things. When I was younger I was taught that being very thin was lovable and beautiful. I was teased and shamed for being overweight by people in my life and my inner critic learned that it wanted to do everything in its power to protect me from ever feeling that shame and judgment. It told me that I needed to control everything around me in order to avoid feeling this shame and guilt. The more I controlled everything, the stronger the inner critic got. I learned that in order to be accepted and feel worthy of love, I needed to please everyone around me. The rules and expectations we take on play a big part in the development of our inner critic. Our inner critic speaks to us about many situations in our lives.

The most recent situation that comes to mind when thinking about the inner critic is something I am currently battling right now. I started writing about two years ago. My writing took off quickly and turned into my first guide which I used to coach a client. That client responded very well to my guide, so I felt compelled to use it with another client. Several clients later, I decided to self-publish the guide and began selling on Amazon. I sold a few copies, but nothing big came of the guide.

Shortly after self-publishing my first book, I began writing my second one called "Renewed: A Mind, Body, Spirit Approach to Self-Renewal". Only this time, my writing was intended to be a book. The book I speak of is the one you are reading right now. While writing the chapters, I also implemented it into a group for teen girls. My teen girls did very well with the content; at least I think they did because they kept coming back.

A few weeks ago, I had a vision of turning this book into a coaching program called "RENEWED". The vision became very clear within a few days and I began to see a program of not just one group, but four. I decided to turn the book I was working on into four separate books which would become a program to address issues with mood, food and relationships.

I got to work quickly and started planning using the table of contents I originally had for both of my books. While the topics were different, the method of healing was the same. I even called my father to ask him for some advice regarding publishing and making my program official. It was after that phone call that the inner critic decided to pay me a visit.

You see, once I started working toward my vision or purpose, feelings of fear and insecurity were triggered. Saying it out loud to other people made my vision real. Saying it out loud meant that there were now expectations of me. Expectations triggered feelings of stress and anxiety. Once the stress and anxiety were triggered, the inner critic came.

My inner critic started slowly by planting thoughts in my head like, "Who do you think you are to be writing all this stuff for people to read?" and "Your writing is no different from anyone else's, so what makes you think this program is going to be any better than anything else out there? What makes you think someone would ever even think about wanting to teach it, let alone buy it?"

About a week into my great idea that started moving forward, I was stopped dead in my tracks. I found myself with no motivation, having difficulty sleeping at night, and struggling to get out of bed. I felt completely disconnected from my intuition. Negativity swept over me like a plague. It was all around. My thoughts became extremely paranoid and now it wasn't just about my writing, but it grew into negative thoughts about who I am and even who my friends were. I began to question everything in my life, including my faith; all because I had a vision and decided to move forward with it. Don't you see? The inner critic starts off with one simple thought and it grows just like our anxiety grows. I believe we feed it. Sometimes we can recognize when we are feeding it and sometimes we can't. Sometimes we can stop it and sometimes we just need to ride it out.

I'm going to be one hundred percent honest with you. I am still battling that nasty critic over this book. But today, I know how to conquer the critic. Today I know and understand why my inner critic is here. Today I know and understand that my inner critic will pass and will leave. My depression will lift once my anxiety lifts. Today I know that it is normal to have an inner critic. I also know that my inner critic is trying to protect me from failure.

Steps to Conquer the Inner Critic

The following are steps I take to overcome my inner critic.

1. **Understand and embrace the *Inner Critic*.** The inner critic is that voice in your head that is constantly asking the "what if's." "What if I can't write this book?" "What if nobody likes it?" "What if it hurts someone?" "What if you cause more harm than good?" "What if?"...."What if?"....."What if?" But I know those are the thoughts my inner critic is telling me.

Think back to chapter one on understanding stress. Anxiety is a feeling triggered by an event or situation that causes a chemical reaction. When a person gets anxious it creates a chemical reaction in our brain. Cortisol rises when we get anxious. Raised cortisol served a purpose for humans and animals back in the day and I truly believe it serves a purpose for us now.

Anxiety was a motivator for survival. No living creature wants to die so we avoid death at all costs. Anxiety and fear created a chemical reaction that released cortisol and other fear producing hormones that motivated humans to access the fight or flight response. It protected people and animals from death by motivating them to gather food and fight for survival. As we evolved our motivators changed but the response did not. The inner critic is actually there to protect us. It asks us the "what if's" and tells us all kinds of irrational things in order to keep us from going out and taking risks or being shamed and judged.

Our inner critic may tell us things like "Don't take the time to put this program together because nobody really cares about your story or what you think or have to say." Or "Everyone thinks you are stupid." Your inner critic may ask you questions like "Who do you think you are?" or "What if you cause more harm than good?" Trust me I can go there too, but I won't because it is not helpful. It is only keeping us from letting go of the fears that bind us and keep us from taking risks; risks that could change someone else's life for the better.

The more we feed the inner critic the stronger it is and the longer it stays around. The inner critic tends to focus on the negative things we hear in the news and on the internet rather the more rational things we hear.

Many times our inner critic judges and shames our feelings. When I started to recognize the fear and insecurity I was feeling, my inner critic started telling me that I should know better by now and should not have those feelings. Crazy, right? Our inner critic is like that parent who thinks if they yell, scream, and punish their child, then the child is going to stop doing what they are doing. This may work temporarily in the moment. Just like a parent trying to protect their child, the inner critic is trying to protect you. But the child isn't going to stop, they are just going to hide it and mask it from the parent. They are going to learn to avoid and shut down in order to avoid feeling shamed or judged or scolded. This is where addictive behaviors come into play. You see, we adopt unhealthy behaviors that gratify our immediate need for pain relief or distract us so we don't have to feel the feelings associated with the inner critic. I used food emotionally to numb and shut off my inner critic. By embracing my inner critic and learning how to assure it that all will be okay, anxiety will decrease.

2. **Access the Inner Coach.** The inner coach is the other little voice in our heads that we tend to ignore. It is the rational voice. You can think of it as the good angel and the bad angel. We all have an inner coach, but as mentioned earlier, every time we focus on the negative and irrational we strengthen the inner critic and weaken the inner coach. Both are like a muscle that needs to be strengthened and trained. Practicing rational self-talk will strengthen your inner coach.

For example, the inner coach says things like, "You've taken many risks in the last couple of years and they've all worked out great," or "Even if you make a mistake and this doesn't work out, you will learn something big from it." Or, how about this one; "You know that your intuition is just going to lead you down another path until you listen to it. It is just going to keep on finding a way to make this book happen." Feed your inner coach, not your inner critic. Accessing the inner coach reassures the inner critic that everything is going to be okay.

3. **Get some help from a spiritual mentor, coach, therapist or friend.** Accessing the inner coach can definitely be a challenge at first. It takes time to build it. It may even take some cuing at first. I still need cuing at times from my supports; someone to prompt me to see the situation differently. Infact, I just called a friend today because I needed to be reminded that the nasty, negative stories I am telling myself are just my inner critic. We will talk more about supports in chapters to come, but for now just know

that it can be very helpful to reach out for help and support when the inner critic is rearing its ugly voice.

4. **Distance yourself from media and people who reinforce irrational thinking and perfectionism.** One of the things I learned throughout my journey with panic, OCD and anxiety is to be mindful of my triggers. Reading about things I am fearful of online and watching things on the news triggers anxiety producing inner critic, irrational thinking which triggers me to emotionally eat. I also learned that I need to surround myself with people who think rationally rather than people who reinforce irrational, inner critic thinking.

5. **Practice staying in the here and now.** One thing I learned about during a long period of severe anxiety and panic followed by months of insomnia was how to stay present in the moment. I was so desperate to make the feelings of tremendous fear and panic go away that I was willing to try anything. So I practiced what I preach, which is mindfulness. Mindfulness is training the mind to be in the present moment.

The minute you begin to experience your inner critic, try asking yourself, "What am I doing right now?" How am I feeling? Am I anxious? What does the anxiety feel like? Does it have a color, a shape or a size? Anxiety is a natural feeling and state of mind. It comes and goes just like any other feeling.

Try reminding yourself that you are FEELING anxiety about a situation, but the situation is not actually happening in the moment. For example, do you remember when the Ebola virus was around in the U.S.? I can't tell you how many clients I had that year due to a rise in anxiety and fear of contracting that virus. It wasn't even near our state and people were panicking. Trust me, I get it. It was a very scary thing to think about. And once or twice my brain did get carried away into thinking about an extreme outbreak and what that would look like. But we never got to the outbreak. That's right! It never happened. So many people suffered anxiety and wasted energy worrying about an outbreak that wasn't even happening. It is okay to have fleeting thoughts, worries and fear, but we can choose to use our inner coach instead of feeding our inner critic.

6. Play the Mindfulness Game. The Mindfulness Game is super simple. You will need your five senses. Here is a sample of the Mindfulness Game. You can play this game with your eyes closed while you are alone or while you are in a busy restaurant or classroom with your eyes open and nobody will even know.

The Mindfulness Game

1. What are 5 things I see with my eyes?

_____
_____
_____
_____
_____

2. What are 5 things I hear with my ears?

_____
_____
_____
_____
_____

3. What are 5 things I taste in my mouth?

_____
_____
_____
_____
_____

4. What are 5 things I smell with my nose?

_____
_____

_____
_____
_____

5. What are 5 things I feel with my skin?

_____
_____
_____
_____
_____

7. **Continue to stay focused on your purpose.** This has helped me tremendously. We all have purpose in our lives. We all have gifts. What do you feel when you are living out your life purpose? When I follow my intuition and live out my purpose, I feel euphoric, happy and at peace. By staying focused on our gifts and purpose we elicit feelings of joy and peace, rather than focusing on something that might happen or worrying about something that we have no control over. When I am focused on my purpose, the inner critic melts away because everything it is telling me really doesn't matter. If I am living my purpose and spending time working on things I am supposed to be working on, things my intuition is leading me toward, then I cannot fail. Even if I make a mistake and go off the path for a bit, I eventually find my way back on.

8. **Practice self-care to manage cortisol levels.** Practicing self-care means making time to do all the things you probably neglect to do because you tell yourself that you don't have time to do them. Life is very busy and fast paced. It can go by in an instant if you let it. It is so crucial that you take the time to slow down and take care of your body, mind and spirit. Self-care skills include, taking time for you to do things that nurture your body, mind and spirit. If you implement self-care into your daily life, then you will keep cortisol levels and other hormones balanced.

Movement can help to flush toxins from the body and release feel good hormones such as serotonin and dopamine. Fueling your body with healthy foods also flushes toxins and keeps our digestion working optimally which also promotes balance. Sleep is very important, so make sure you get to bed at a decent time and get adequate rest. Practicing yoga and meditation strengthen awareness and the muscles in the brain that work to benefit a healthy body, mind and spirit. Going out with friends and laughing releases feel good hormones. These are all examples of self-care.

These skills do not come easily and they do not happen overnight. Remember, the brain is a muscle and needs to be trained like a muscle through repetition.

9. **Practice Self-Compassion.** In order to heal from inner critic shame and abuse, we must learn self-compassion. This includes using the inner coach to rationalize our thoughts. But it also includes being kind and loving to ourselves regardless of what our minds are telling us. Practicing self-compassion is the biggest way to overcome our inner critic thinking.

Challenges You May Face

There are two big challenges to conquering the inner critic.

1. **It takes patience.** As I've stated many times thus far, changing our thought patterns takes time. There is no quick fix for this kind of change. It takes series of ups and downs in order to re-learn new ways of thinking, doing and being.

2. **You must take risks and make mistakes in order to learn from them.** By learning how to conquer the inner critic and access our inner coach, we begin to let go of perfectionism. Many people struggle with the expectation that we have to be perfect. We have to do our purpose perfectly. We have to live our life perfectly. We tell ourselves that we are not

allowed to mess up and make mistakes. Why? Because messing up triggers stress and we don't like to feel stress. So we live our lives expecting perfection in ourselves and others. I think some of these messages were planted in our brains when we were young and some we've learned along the way. They are cultural and societal messages.

So Now What?

Take some time to reflect on your inner thoughts. What are the stories you tell yourself? Practice self-compassion by allowing yourself to be human and make mistakes. I don't know about you, but some of my greatest and most important lessons in my life come from mistakes I made. I am one stubborn human being. I don't learn the easy way. Unfortunately, I like to do things my way. And most of the time, my way, which is intended to be the easy way, turns out to be the complicated, hard way. But you know what? Today I am okay with that. I am okay with it because at least I am trying it in the first place. While I am learning how to surrender and do things God's way, I know that if I mess up, then He will fix it for me. He always does.

Questions for Reflection

Find a quiet space where there are little to no distractions. Take a moment in quiet to reflect on what you just read. When you are ready, answer the following questions in your journal.

1. What are some people, places and things in your life that trigger your inner critic?

2. What are some of the stories your inner critic tells you?

3. Do you recognize your inner coach? What might your inner coach say to your inner critic regarding your answers in number 2?

4. How does your inner critic keep you from surrendering your anxiety and perfectionism? How does it keep you from living your purpose?

5. List any coaches, mentors, friends or therapists who can assist you when your inner critic is present?

6. Do you have negative people, places, or things in your life that reinforce negative thoughts such as the news, social media, friends, etc.? Please explain.

7. The next time you feel the inner critic is present, practice the mindfulness game to help reduce anxiety and cortisol. Take a moment to reflect on this experience. Describe it. Did it work?

8. As you learned, as cortisol rises due to increased anxiety, our bodies can become chemically unbalanced. What are some self-care strategies you can implement into your life to keep cortisol levels low (Diet, movement, sleep, etc)?

Chapter Six

Understanding Grief and Learning Self-Compassion

"Acceptance is fully letting go of the expectations in a situation and embracing them without trying to fix or change them."

One of the biggest lessons I learned on this journey is how to grieve loss and change in my life and find acceptance. I had these silent expectations that I projected onto myself and others; expectations that I learned in my society, culture, family and religion, of what I thought my life was supposed to be about or how it was supposed to play out. These expectations kept me from embracing change. I had expectations of who I was supposed to be and how I was supposed to be. I had expectations of the people, places and things around me. In order to let go of those expectations and embrace the changes in my life, I had to learn acceptance; therefore, I had to learn how to grieve.

Take a moment to think about your life. Are you in the midst of any kind of change? Are you grieving a loss in your life, whether it be a person, place, expectation or desire? And lastly, how does it feel?

There are so many feelings associated with grief. The only feeling that feels good is when we finally reach the acceptance stage. Grief is a process that includes the following stages: denial, anger, bargaining/guilt/shame, sadness/depression and acceptance. Grieving is a healthy human process. We can get stuck in grief because it feels bad and instead of having self-compassion, we judge or shame ourselves.

This chapter will provide some education on the stages of grief. By learning how to identify and understand our feelings, especially with regard to grief, we are able to have self-compassion, rather than judgment, shame or guilt. By having self-compassion, we are able to surrender those feelings and move through our grief, rather than getting stuck in the midst of the denial, anger, bargaining, shame, guilt or sadness.

Expectations and Change

Today I recognize that my life is always changing, therefore, I am always grieving. People are always coming and going. I've experienced job changes, friendship changes, changes in my family relationships and changes within myself. But I spent most of my life avoiding or resisting change; fighting or flighting. I held onto expectations and the shoulds and should nots, until I realized that fighting and flighting was keeping me stuck.

An expectation is a story we create in our mind and then project onto a person, place, thing or situation. An expectation is the "should" and "shouldn't" we recite in our minds. One thing I know for sure is that expectations lead to disappointment and resentment, which keeps us from living a peaceful and harmonious life. Therefore, we need to let go of our expectations. But how do we let go of our expectations and surrender the "shoulds" and "should nots" in our stories? The answer is by learning how to grieve them.

Grief

What do you think of when you hear the word "grief"? When

I ask this question, most people tend to answer "death". While we experience grief with death, we also experience grief with life. Grief is the process that leads to acceptance. Acceptance happens when we let go of something. It can include letting go of the passing of a loved one. It can include letting go of a job. It can include letting go of a friendship. It can include letting go of an idea or vision. It can include letting go of a desire or expectation. You see, we experience grief on a weekly basis. We just don't realize it.

DENIAL

Denial is the first stage of grief. It is the inability to see what needs to be changed or accepted. Often times we assume that denial means that a person doesn't want to see what needs to be accepted or changed. But the real issue is that they are not ready.

For years I lived in denial about my family dysfunction. I grew up thinking my family was perfect. I started having a lot of issues in high school and college and still could not see how or where those issues started. I blamed everyone else for my problems because I was in denial. I thought my relationships were struggling because of the other person. I thought my eating disorder developed because I had a low self-esteem. I thought my anxiety was normal.

I will never forget the first time I came to the realization that my family had problems. I was a junior in college and was taking a class called, "Dysfunctional Family Therapy." We were watching a movie on family addiction when about three quarters of the way through the movie it hit me like a ton of bricks. My affect got flat and I just sat there dazed and confused. The wheels in my head began to spin. I thought I was going to be sick.

I went home that evening and sobbed. For the first time, I could see my family dynamics clearly. The denial was removed and I could see the dysfunction. The family roles we all played were exposed and the impact all of this had on me became clear. I was so confused by how I could go so long not understanding or knowing this. It was then that I realized that my family was normal to me. It was all that I knew. I wasn't ready to see my family dynamics for what they were because I was still trying to just survive them.

When we are triggered by stress, our nervous system goes into survival mode and we fight, flight or freeze. Survival mode distracts and blocks our ability to see. It creates blind spots. We do not become ready to see beyond those blind spots until we begin to feel safe. In order to move through denial and into the second stage of grief, we must be able to identify the problem and see beyond the blind spots.

The beautiful thing is that we have a precious gift called time. Having time means that we don't need to uncover all of our issues today. Therefore, we cannot expect ourselves or others to.

Having self-compassion means understanding the purpose for denial and allowing ourselves the time needed to feel safe enough to come out of survival mode. It is then and only then that we will see what needs to be seen in order to move through our denial. We all have blind spots. Blind spots protect us. Self-compassion is accepting that those blind spots will be revealed when they are supposed to be revealed in Gods time.

ANGER AND RESENTMENT
Anger is the second stage of grief. Often times we experience anger toward ourselves, another person, or God during times of grief. Anger can lead to blaming and feelings of resentment. The anger stage can last anywhere from a few minutes to several years.

I find anger fascinating. I spent so many years feeling angry and resentful toward many different people. I got stuck in my anger and resentment and it impacted my relationship with myself and others. Anger is not a very pleasant feeling. It triggered and fueled my eating disorder. I used food to cope with these feelings instead of understanding that feeling angry is normal and then allowing it to pass. I judged, shamed and hated myself for feeling angry.

Once I realized my family problems, I became angry. I was angry at my grandmother and also angry at my parents because they allowed my grandmother to do the things she did in our family. I felt angry that nobody would listen and I felt angry that they didn't change it. I didn't realize that my denial was lifted, but theirs wasn't. I had the expectation that just because I could now see the dysfunction, that they should now be able to see it too. I was also angry because I was grieving what my childhood "should" have been. I had expectations that were not met and I was angry and resentful which impacted my relationship with my family for years. I lost years with my family because I did not understand my grief.

We all get angry at times. When I meet with someone and they express anger, I simply listen and validate their feelings of anger. Their anger cues me to ask them about their expectations. You see, when we feel angry, it is very likely that there is some kind of expectation we've put on a person, place or thing. And when those expectations are not met, then we get angry and resentful. We need to understand that anger is a part of grieving and that in order to reach acceptance, we must release our expectations.

Self-compassion allows us to examine our expectations without judgement or shame. It allows us to recognize and normalize our feelings of anger and resentment which allows us to let go of the expectations we have in the situation. It allows us to also have compassion toward another person's grief.

BARGAINING, SHAME OR GUILT

The third stage of grief is where we experience bargaining, shame and guilt. During this stage we ask ourselves the "what if's". We play through scenarios in our heads and punish ourselves emotionally by shaming and guilting ourselves into thinking we could have done something different.

Bargaining is another normal stage in grief. In order to move toward acceptance, it is likely that we will encounter some guilt and shame. Just like anger, guilt and shame do not feel good. And when something doesn't feel good we tend to try to fix it or block it out. Many people become stuck in this stage because they are unable to accept and move through the guilt and shame feelings.

As I began to work through my feelings regarding my family, I began to let go of the anger. Once the anger melted, I began to experience feelings of bargaining. This included the "What if" scenarios. "What if I got help for myself earlier? What if I was stronger? What if my grandmother changed? If I do this…then maybe they will get it. If I tell them this…then maybe they will change."

Bargaining set me up to have expectations again and therefore spiraled me right back into the anger stage which triggered more guilt and shame for being angry.

If I had an understanding of my grief, then I would have known that I was in the bargaining stage. I would have known that my feelings of guilt and shame were a normal part of grieving my childhood and my expectations. But I didn't understand my grief and in turn got stuck for years harboring feelings of guilt and shame.

It wasn't until I learned to have self-compassion that I learned how to accept and embrace these feelings and this stage of grief. Self-compassion allows us to identify bargaining, shame and guilt as a normal and healthy stage that we must go through in order to accept something that is difficult for us to accept. Having self-compassion allows us to take care of ourselves while we are feeling these ugly feelings instead of punishing or beating ourselves up more.

SADNESS AND DEPRESSION

The fourth stage in the grief process is sadness and depression. Depression is when a person experiences extreme bouts of sadness, anger, or irritability followed by feelings of hopelessness and discouragement. A person may experience sadness and depression on many different levels.
It's been my experience both personally and professionally that the sadness and depression stage can fluctuate back and forth among anger, bargaining and depression several times before finally reaching the acceptance stage.

I experienced a long period of sadness and depression during the grieving of my family. I can remember feeling several different layers of sadness at different times. I can remember the sadness fluctuating back and forth with anger and bargaining. And I can even look back and remember denial being lifted several different times throughout the course of my grief.

During the depression stage, I was still able to function, but I was angry, irritable and controlling. I fell deep into my eating disorder during my depression stage of grief. I used food to numb the feelings of sadness so I did not have to feel them.

I was able to work through my grief, but it took many years and I feel like I lost so much because of the amount of time it took. Looking back, I can see that I did not understand my grief. I hurt people during my grief and I also hurt myself because I did not know how to live through the grief in a healthy way.

Today I understand sadness and depression and I know that it is a normal stage of grief. When I feel sad or depressed about something I am able to ask myself if there is something I am grieving or need to let go of; some kind of expectation I need to release. Every time I do this, the answer is yes.

Self-compassion allows me to understand my sadness and depression by allowing me the time and space it takes to work through the sadness. Self-compassion allows me to rest more often because when I am sad, I get tired more easily. Self-compassion allows me to talk about my feelings and express them without labeling myself "too sensitive" or "ridiculous" for feeling that way. Self-compassion allows me to go inward and take more time for myself during periods of sadness and depression; it gives me permission to say "no" to people places and things so I can give myself the space I need to grieve.

ACCEPTANCE

Acceptance is fully letting go of expectations in a situation and embracing it without trying to fix or change it. It is the final stage of the grief. A person can experience acceptance for a period of time, then regress back to previous stages of grief such as anger, bargaining or depression. There are many levels of acceptance within one situation.

"And acceptance is the answer to all my problems today. When I am disturbed, it is because I find some person, place, thing, or situation-some fact of my life-unacceptable to me and I can find no serenity until I accept that person, place, thing, or situation as being exactly how it is supposed to be at this moment. Nothing, absolutely nothing, happens in God's world by mistake." (Big Book of Alcoholics Anonymous, Bill Wilson).

I live my life seeking acceptance in every day. But in order to accept each day as being exactly as it is supposed to be, I grieve. I go through the stages of grief on a weekly basis and sometimes don't even realize it. My mood fluctuates on a weekly basis because of this grief.

I will never forget the day I walked into my psychiatrist's office sobbing. He looked at me and asked me why I was crying. I explained to him that I just came from dropping my youngest son off to preschool. It was recommended that my 5 year old start preschool that year due to his speech delays. None of my other children went to preschool. They all started school in kindergarten. I was a stay at home mom who worked part-time in the afternoons and on weekends, so preschool was not something in my parenting plan; it was not something I expected. Regardless of whether it was expected or not, I was experiencing grief because of a major change in my life. I was home with children full-time for 8 years straight. And that was the first day in 8 years that I was without children. I was grieving.

The psychiatrist immediately began increasing my dose of medication. I was so confused because I knew in my heart that the feelings I was having were normal. It was that day that my denial was lifted and I could see the gaps in traditional medicinal thinking. It was that day that I began to reassess my decision to be on medication for my mood. It was that day that I began the process of grieving my life and seeking acceptance in myself and others. It was that day that I began to understand grief and how it impacted my mood on a day to day basis. It was that day that I began to have self-compassion instead of judgment.

How to Grieve by Practicing Self-Compassion

Self-compassion is accepting and allowing yourself to be exactly who you are in the present moment. It is allowing yourself permission to feel all of the uncomfortable feelings associated with grief without judgement, shame or guilt. Self-compassion allows us to let go of perfectionism. Self-compassion allows us to let go of expectations. It allows us to let go of anger and resentment toward ourselves and others. It allows us to accept others by grieving our expectations. It allows us to do all of this without putting a label on ourselves and without trying to fix or change ourselves.

The following are ways to have self-compassion:

1. **Give yourself time and space to feel emotions and grieve without judgement, shame or guilt.**

2. **Talk to a friend who can listen without judgement.**

3. **Write in a journal and wrestle through your feelings of grief.**

4. **Educate yourself about grief and self-compassion.**

5. **Set healthy boundaries and say "no" to things you don't have the energy to do.**

6. **Limit your time and energy on social media.**

7. **Limit your time with toxic people, places and things and surround yourself with people who are on a similar spiritual journey.**

8. **Take time to be with God in prayer and meditation. Pray for acceptance and peace.**

9. **Get adequate amounts of sleep, eat well and drink plenty of water.**

10. **Practice self-acceptance by acknowledging your feelings and using positive self-talk to remind yourself that you are healthy and normal for feeling your grief.**

So What Now?

Take a moment to reflect on your expectations. What are the stories you create in your mind and project onto yourself or others? Instead of holding on to what you think should or should not be, let the expectations go by allowing yourself to experience grief. Practice self-compassion with yourself by loving and nurturing yourself. Doing this will not only heal your grief, but will allow you to feel peace during the grieving process.

Questions for Reflection

Find a quiet space where there are little to no distractions.
Take a moment in quiet to reflect on what you just read.
When you are ready, answer the following questions in your
journal.

1. After reading this chapter, do you recognize any areas of your life where you may be experiencing grief? Please make a list of the people, places, things or situations you may be grieving.

2. For each person, place, thing or situation you are grieving, identify what stage or stages of grief you are experiencing with each one.

3. For each person, place, thing or situation you are grieving, please list your expectations ("should" or "should nots") for each of them, including expectations you have for yourself.

4. For each person, place, thing, or situation you are grieving, please make a list of ways you can have self-compassion while working through your grief using the list of ways above.

5. What are 3 positive things you can remind yourself as you are grieving?

Chapter Seven

Boundaries

"Our intuition tells us when to set a boundary, but a boundary allows us to find and honor our true self and live out our purpose in life. Without boundaries, we will spend our time and energy pleasing others."

In order to live an intuitive life and practice self-care we must have boundaries. Boundaries draw lines spiritually, emotionally, mentally and physically to protect us, keep us safe and help us to reserve our energy so we can use it toward our life purpose.

I was taught boundaries growing up, but not all of them were healthy ones. Some of them were confusing. We live in a people pleasing society where many of us are so afraid to say "no" or set limits with others. Many people in our society don't know how to accept boundaries. We become easily offended if someone tells us "no" or tries to set a limit with us. As a result, we learn that boundaries are bad because they don't always feel comfortable.

We raise our children to follow directions, but we go overboard by teaching them to ignore their intuition, instincts and feelings by shaming them when they tell us "no" or try to communicate their boundaries with us. We live with all or nothing thinking, rather than living intuitively. Instead of guiding our children, we tell them what to do, what not to do, how to feel, how not to feel, what to think and what not to think. Just like expectations, we instill our beliefs about boundaries onto them instead of guiding them to establish their own.

Please do not misunderstand me. Children do NEED boundaries. They require healthy boundaries to keep them physically and emotionally safe. But as they grow older, just like the rules and expectations we talked about in chapter four, those boundaries need to evolve depending upon the mental, emotional, physical and spiritual needs of each child. The boundaries and limits I set with my 12 year old may be different from the boundaries and limits I set with my 9 year old because they are different people with different needs. And sometimes those boundaries will be the same.

Healthy Boundaries vs. Unhealthy Boundaries

As I began my journey with intuitive living I learned the importance of setting healthy boundaries. I learned what I needed in order to maintain balance. I learned how to listen to my mind, body and spirit and I learned to set limits with people, places and things around me. I learned to identify what I am okay with and what I am not okay with by acknowledging my feelings in a situation and the consequences of my behaviors. I learned to identify what I needed from others and what I didn't need from others. I learned how to say "no" and how to ask for help. Most of all I learned how to not take offense when someone gets upset with me for setting a limit or boundary; I learned to not internalize or take their reaction personally.

Setting healthy boundaries is necessary if we are going to live an intuitive life. Our intuition tells us when we need to set a boundary, but a boundary allows us to find and honor our true self and live out our purpose in life. Without boundaries, we will spend our time and energy pleasing others. Without boundaries, we become enmeshed in our relationships and we are at risk for becoming co-dependent with others or at risk for being taken advantage of.

Part of my healing has been through learning to set boundaries. I not only needed to look at the boundaries in my relationships, but I also needed to look at my boundaries in terms of my priorities and pleasure. I find that life goes smoothly when it is balanced. Too little or too much of anything is usually not a good thing. The following are examples of healthy boundaries.

- Taking things slowly rather than rushing into them.
- Staying focused on your goals and purpose rather than becoming distracted by negativity, drama and chaos.
- Exploring the consequences before making a decision whether it be with a person, place or thing.
- Honoring your own personal values and being who you are rather than changing them to please someone else's.
- Being able to give and receive.
- Being able to say stop or say "no" when something doesn't feel right.
- Being able to ask for help without guilt, shame or resentment.
- Trusting your own intuition and not depending on the reassurance of others.
- Understanding that all humans are flawed and will let us down at some point. They cannot read our minds.
- Accepting others and being accepted by others.
- Not chasing after friends.
- Knowing when enough is enough and being able to put up limits or make changes when needed.
- Being able to recognize when someone else displays inappropriate boundaries.
- Maintaining balance and not being consumed by one person, place or thing.

Challenges to Setting Healthy Boundaries in Relationships

Once I was able to recognize unhealthy relationships, I began to learn how to set appropriate boundaries with those people. Setting boundaries was not and is still not an easy task for me. I love people and I have a hard time understanding the behaviors and intentions of other people. I learned along the way that different people have different personalities based on their life story. Some personalities can be harmful and toxic to my well-being; draining my energy that is needed for good. Some people stir up drama and trouble and have learned to depend on that chaos to meet their needs. Some people struggle with attention seeking behaviors and will exaggerate, lie, cheat and manipulate to get their needs met. Some will go out of their way to hurt others just to get a reaction even if it is a negative one.

These kind of characteristics in people triggered fears and insecurities in me, making it difficult for me to say "no" to them or distance myself from the relationship. The following are some of the challenges we can expect to face while preparing and setting healthy boundaries with people, places or things:

1. **We may experience feelings of fear as the result of preparing to set a boundary.** We fear abandonment and rejection from the person we are setting the boundary with. And we fear what others think of us for setting a limit or boundary.

2. **We may experience feelings guilt or shame after setting a boundary.** Often times we bargain while making the decision to set a limit or boundary. We begin second guessing ourselves whether or not we should or should not set the boundary. We can lose time, energy and sleep during this process.

3. **We can experience retaliation.** Sometimes people get angry when a limit or boundary is set and they retaliate by trying to hurt us emotionally and sometimes even physically.

4. **We can experience loss and rejection.** Sometimes we lose a friendship when we begin to set limits and boundaries with a person. If that person is in your life because they seek relationships where there are enmeshed or rigid boundaries, then they may become stressed and flee the relationship when a boundary is set.

Ways to Set Appropriate Boundaries in Relationships

Setting limits and boundaries is a challenge and can cause fear, anxiety, insecurity and trigger stress. Remember what happens when we experience stress. Our body goes into fight, flight or freeze mode which usually triggers very uncomfortable feelings. This is why many people have trouble setting limits and boundaries in the first place. We either get defensive or we avoid setting limits all together. The following is a list of ways to set appropriate boundaries:

- Keep a healthy distance in relationships both physically and emotionally; don't become too enmeshed.
- Be clear and to the point; keep the limit short and sweet.
- Stay focused on the limit and don't get caught up in an argument. Set the boundary, then stop talking.
- Be aware of what you are posting on social media and what your privacy settings are set to with your audience.
- Know yourself by knowing what you are comfortable with and what you are not comfortable with, then honor it.
- Always acknowledge your feelings in a situation or relationship; do not judge them or dismiss them.
- Know that it is okay to say "NO" without feeling guilt or shame.

- Honor your feelings before honoring the feelings of the other person. What you have left to offer, you can give.
- Set one limit at a time.
- Get support and validation from your healthy support system.

So Now What?

I look at my life today, several years later, and I am so grateful that I continued on a spiritual path. I am grateful for the many personalities and different people I've encountered and grateful for the lessons I've learned. I am so grateful for the people God put into my life and the people who continue to surround me today. I am still learning how to set and maintain healthy boundaries and I still struggle with the grief of old relationships, but today I am okay with where my relationships are. I have gained deeper, more supportive relationships with people who understand me and my needs. Some relationships are here for a short season and some will be here with me for a lifetime. I no longer fear rejection like I used to because I understand that there is a purpose and place for every person who enters my life and I trust that God will provide those relationships when needed and exactly how they are needed.

Questions for Reflection

Find a quiet space where there are little to no distractions. Take a moment in quiet to reflect on what you just read. When you are ready, answer the following questions in your journal.

1. What kinds of boundaries can you remember being introduced to as a child? Were they healthy or unhealthy? How did/do they impact your boundaries today?

2. After reading this chapter, do you recognized any unhealthy boundaries in your life today whether it be with a person, place or thing? How do you know they are unhealthy?

3. After reading this chapter, do you recognize any healthy boundaries in your life today whether it be with a person, place or thing? How do you know they are healthy?

4. What are the challenges you face when thinking about setting limits and boundaries in your life?

5. What are the areas in your life that you are you willing to set healthier limits and boundaries?

6. What are some ways you can begin to set healthy boundaries in your life today specifically in the areas listed in number 5?

Chapter Eight

Building a Healthy Support System

"Letting go of the toxic relationships allows time, space and energy for new and more positive relationships."

Having a healthy support system is necessary if I am going to be successful with intuitive living. A healthy support system is a network of people who you can turn to for help, encouragement and emotional support. I found that I need supports that are positive and can help me to see the blessings in a situation, rather ones who can only see the negative in a situation. I need supports that are able to provide a safe space and listening ear so I can explore my feelings without shame or judgement. I need supports that can help me by offering to watch my children so I can practice self-care. I need supports that are able to foster spiritual growth and guidance by gently challenging my unhealthy thinking.

Mentally and spiritually healthy people are not always easy to come by. Another challenge I faced in my life was relating to others. Throughout my journey of healing and growth, I learned so much about people and relationships. And as I stated before, I learned about the importance of healthy boundaries. I guess I didn't realize that parts of my support system were broken and unhealthy. I learned that I was in relationships with narcissistic people, negative people, selfish people, and people that were not able to respect my limits and boundaries.

My relationships were one-sided and I took on the role of trying to take care of and fix others. I put this responsibility on myself. I was drawn to people that I could pity. I needed to be needed and felt a sense of fulfillment when I was needed. I needed approval from others and avoided abandonment at all cost by sacrificing my needs to please others. I was rigid and had difficulty adjusting to change, trouble identifying my emotions. I had a lack of trust in both myself and others and difficulty asserting myself by saying "no" and asking for help. If I was upset in a relationship, I kept quiet to keep the peace because I feared the other person being mad at me and ending the relationship. Unfortunately I engaged with people who did reject me if I spoke up. I felt compelled to control the people, places and things around me because it felt safer and I knew what to expect. I was co-dependent in these relationships.

Understanding and Breaking Free from Co-dependency

I talk much about my "spiritual awakening" where I was at my bottom and forced to make some pretty big changes in my life; specifically with regard to my boundaries and breaking free from co-dependency. I believe that we can have more than one awakening. But during this particular awakening, I began a deeper and more spiritual relationship with God. During this awakening, I learned that depending on others resulted with me feeling hurt and disappointed. Why? Because ALL people are flawed, just like me.

I expected perfection from others. I expected them to be able to fully understand me at all times and got upset and felt rejected when they couldn't. It wasn't until I became fully dependent on God, that I was able to break free from my co-dependency with others.

I believe we are all co-dependent in some ways. We rely and depend on people, places and things to make us happy. And when they fail, we get upset. Breaking free from co-dependency meant building healthy relationships without relying on or depending on others to fulfill or make me happy.

It meant letting go or setting boundaries with those whose behaviors left me feeling drained and constantly stressed. Building healthy relationships meant wanting people in my life rather than needing them and being able to accept those people for exactly who they are; flaws and all.

Because I was co-dependent, certain personalities were drawn to me. I tended to draw narcissistic, manipulative, gamey and selfish people. Narcissists could feed off my giving nature and could take advantage of me. They would begin a relationship by creating a space where I felt needed, wanted and special. Then they would manipulate me by taking advantage of my caring and empathic tendencies to feed themselves, knowing that I would become dependent and chase them for their love. They took advantage of my kindness and fed off of my negative reactions toward them. They craved the game and the attention and I craved their love. I lived in this cycle with people most of my life. It became an addictive pattern.

Needy people were also drawn to me because I was always so willing to jump in and try to fix and save the day. Needy people would always want and expect me to give more and more emotionally to them until I could not give anymore. Needy people tended to be negative and emotionally exhausting. They perceived everything as a crisis and expected me to perceive the situations the same way and expected me to provide care and support as one would in a crisis. These people were not bad people. In fact, these kinds of people were some of my favorite people, I simply did not know how to relate to them in a healthy way. I would sacrifice my self-care to help those who needed me and I fed off of being needed and wanted. But eventually, I felt drained and stuck in relationships where no matter how much I gave, it was never enough. I eventually realized that I didn't set healthy boundaries from the start and that my giving was never going to fulfill the other person's needs because their issues stemmed from something deeper.

Throughout my journey I came to the realization that some of my emotional eating, well actually most of my emotional eating, was deeply triggered by the dysfunction in these relationships. Over time, my emotional eating became addictive just like my relationships became addictive. My addictions forced me to change my negative patterns and ways with myself and others. My addictions led me to learn about co-dependency, narcissism and other unhealthy personalities that surrounded my life. Healing my addictions led me to find new supports; healthier supports, set healthier boundaries with people and finally break free from my co-dependent ways.

Who are the Supports in my Life?

While it is not my place to analyze, diagnose, figure out, understand or judge people, I do feel that it is my responsibility to recognize certain behaviors in the people in my life and how those behaviors impact my physical, mental, emotional and spiritual well-being. By recognizing a person's behaviors and how they impact my well-being, I am able to assess where to set the boundary in the relationship.

Today I am learning that I DO NOT NEED to assume or understand the intentions of others, but I DO NEED to assess how their behaviors impact my physical, mental, emotional and spiritual well-being and honor myself by setting healthy limits and boundaries with those individuals.

My support system today is full of many different people, places and things. It changes all the time depending on where I am in my spiritual journey. But one thing remains the same. I seek positive energy in my relationships and flee from negativity in relationships. It is important to note that the people in a support system are human beings. They have flaws and defects just like me, so it is just as important for me to love and accept them for who they are. I find that if I stay focused on the positive energy in the relationship, then it can be used as a very healthy and positive support system. The following is a list of the types of supports I currently have in my life.

1. **Immediate Family Supports.** My immediate family consists of my biggest support, my husband. My husband supports me by listening to me and providing a space for me to explore and express my thoughts and feelings. He is gentle and loving; not critical or judgmental. He is wise and rational most of the time, which is helpful too. We are able to have disagreements and respect each other's opinions without having to compromise our own thoughts or beliefs.

I also have my three children ages 12, 10 and 9. My children support me in so many ways as well. As a mother, it is easy to get caught up in the care-taking role and ignore my self-care. I've talked with my children about the importance of "Mommy taking care of herself". I explain to them all of the ways that I do it. They see me practice intuitive living. They see me pray to God. They see me go to church and participate in small groups for support, encouragement and growth. They see me go on weekend retreats to continue to learn how I can improve myself and continue on my path of spiritual growth. They see me exercise almost daily. They see me nourish my body with healthy food choices. They support me going to my yoga class once a week.

They get sad when I leave the house, especially when I go on my retreats, but they see how peaceful it makes me. They see that it makes me a better mom to them. Modeling self-care has had a tremendous impact on them.

2. **Extended Family Supports.** My extended family consists of parents, siblings, in-laws, cousins, aunts and uncles. They don't always understand me, but they listen to me, encourage me and support me the best way they know how. There are always there in a crisis and they are huge

supports with my kids. My mom has become one of my best listeners and greatest supports. I can always count on her to validate me and show me love and empathy when I need it.

3. **Church Supports.** One of the biggest changes I made in my life was the decision to leave the church I grew up in. I feel incredibly connected and supported at church today. I know that if I needed something that my church family would be there to support me. There was a week that I was struggling quite a bit and could not make it to church because my kids were ill and a church friend asked if I needed her to come watch them, so that I could go. I've never had anyone offer to help me like that before. She barely knew me at the time and I just thought it was so incredibly kind and caring. My church friends have been amazing. They are so eager to help, listen and lend a hand. They give great spiritual guidance and they keep me grounded. They are always helping me to see God's work in a situation rather the negativity.

4. **Occupational Supports.** My work environment changed so much in the last two years. I went from a large, corporate work environment to a small, private practice. I can honestly say that I feel so much more support on my own than I ever did in a large setting. I met some other mental health professionals along the way and one day I was guided spiritually to set up some peer collaboration groups. I now run two clinical support groups for myself and others. I also absolutely love my clients. Although we have a working relationship, sometimes I feel closer to my clients than I do with my own family. This is because our relationship is spiritually based. Although we do not hang out and I do not go to my clients with my problems or to seek advice, I know that if anything tragic happened to me or my family that my clients would be the first to offer support.

5. **Social Supports.** I have old friends and I have new friends. I am slowly learning that friends come and go. I am learning that there is a natural flow of energy in this world. And if I just let go of trying to control the flow of that energy, then the people, places and things that are meant to be in my life or taken out of my life will be exactly as they are supposed to be. I am learning that I may not always understand the reasons for relationships ending, but I am learning to trust that there is a reason, season and purpose for everything and everyone. As I grow spiritually, my relationships also grow. My relationships are becoming more supportive, more intimate and much healthier; much less codependent. I found this lesson to be the most painful one, but the one that has taught me the most spiritually. I continue to trust and let go of the fears and anxiety I have in relationships, knowing that I will forever be provided for by God. He knows everything about me. He will protect me from the harm of others if I move and get out of His way; if I stop trying to control everything.

6. **Medical and Healthcare Providers.** During my spiritual journey the last few years I made a decision to change primary care doctor. I recognized that although I admire my old doctor very much, she was simply overbooked and not able to provide the type of care and attention I needed. I wanted a more personable relationship with my primary care doctor. I was also seeking someone who could be open to a holistic approach. Changing providers was another scary change for me, but it turned out to be a very positive change. I also have a chiropractor who is like a spiritual mother to me. She has been part of my life since I was 22 years old. She is one of the people in my life who God has blessed me with for a lifetime.

7. **Community Support.** Lastly, I consider the places my family are involved in to be support systems. I pick places such as martial arts studios, yoga studios, gyms and sports arenas that are supportive, dependable and reliable. I look

for people and places that are open to learning about my family's needs and interests and ones who can provide support and encouragement. I pick people and places that foster positive energy rather than negative energy. Some of these places have become like family to us.

What Do I Look for in a Support System?

In order to do all the things in this guide that I've written about, I needed support and encouragement. I needed understanding and love. I needed people who could accept me, not judge me. I needed supportive people who could offer help so I could have the time to take care of my spiritual needs. As I began to let go of control in my life, I was given the gift of support. The following is a list of things I look for in a support system today.

1. **I look for supports who can love me unconditionally.** Unconditional love means that the relationship is able to go through ups and downs. Unconditional love is loving someone even when you don't understand or agree with them. Unconditional love is accepting one's flaws and character defects and loving them no matter what.

2. **I look for supports that are non-judgmental and accepting.** I am a very unique person with complex thoughts, feelings and ideas. I am very passionate and can be somewhat impulsive at times, especially in times where I have high anxiety or excitement. I need supports that are not going to make me feel judged and shamed. I need supports that can accept my flaws and not gossip behind my back.

3. **I look for supports that are open-minded.** Open-minded people tend to be less judgmental and open to changes in the relationship. I look for supports that are able to be flexible and open to my growth and able to flow with it. I

seek people who do not control or manipulate. I seek people who do not cause unnecessary drama.

4. **I look for supports that are on a spiritual journey.** As I continue to seek spiritual growth, I am finding that others who are on a similar path can love and accept me unconditionally. They are working toward a deeper spiritual level just like me and are more open to try to understand me, rather judge and reject me. These supports are also able to guide me spiritually and help me to foster positive energy rather than negative energy. Supports that are on a spiritual journey are also more likely to set appropriate boundaries in relationships as well as accept boundaries without internalizing them and becoming angry.

5. **I look for supports that are able to give and receive.** For the longest time I had so much trouble receiving. This caused so many problems for me. I engaged in relationships where I was giving all the time. I was either watching someone's children, making them dinner, or listening to their problems. But I was never able to reach out for their support. It was very uncomfortable for me to ask for help. This was something I was not taught to do and it felt very shameful when I did do it. I always felt like in order to receive help, I needed to first be the helper.

I began to find myself depleted in relationships and left with feelings of resentment. Little did I know that I contributed to this dynamic because of my inability to receive. As I changed this behavior, I found that some of my friends did not need me anymore and were not as interested in a relationship. I had to let them go in order to find healthier supports that were able to give and receive. I had to practice asking for help without feeling like I had to owe somebody. I learned from a very wise woman that I had to allow my need for help to be someone else's "blessing " or "gift" of giving.

6. **I look for supports that are able to provide a safe space for me process negativity.** These supports may be a spiritual

group, therapist, mentor, close friend or family member. They are able to listen without judgment and criticism and they are able to sit with my feelings, rather than fix them or make them go away. They do not reject me if I am unable to give of myself. And they challenge me in a positive and loving way.

So Now What?

Today I understand that some of the people, places and things in my support system were toxic; they were holding me back from my spiritual growth. They were triggering feelings of shame, guilt, and anxiety, which triggered my desire to use food for comfort. I was codependent in my relationships, always seeking to please and fix others and depended on this type of relationship to feel worthy. I depended on them to make me happy and feel fulfilled and when they couldn't live up to this expectation, then I became angry, lonely and depressed. I also recognized that due to my tendency to internalize EVERYTHING, I had much difficulty accepting people, places and things for who and how they were. Instead, I internalized many things and created negativity around me.

I continue to let go of the negative people in my life by grieving them. Letting go of toxic relationships allows time, space and energy for new and more positive relationships. If a person, place or thing begins to stir up negative energy, then I take a step back and reflect on where the energy needs to shift. Sometimes it means walking completely away from the relationship and sometimes it means setting some boundaries. Either way, it means that I need to make some changes. The process has been extremely scary, painful and even confusing at times. But as I continue to let go and let the natural spiritual power take over, I am forever amazed at the outcome.

Take some time to assess your relationships with the people in your life. Begin to explore ways that you can create and build your healthy support system. Allow yourself to let go of negative people, places and things by embracing grief and practicing acceptance.

Questions for Reflection

Find a quiet space where there are little to no distractions. Take a moment in quiet to reflect on what you just read. When you are ready, answer the following questions in your journal.

1. What are your current support systems (people, places and things)? You can choose from the list of supports above and/or add your own.

2. Take out a blank sheet of paper and draw a line down the middle. On the left side make a list of your supports (people, places and things) that foster positivity. On the right make a list of your supports that foster negativity. Explain. (Some supports may fall into both categories and that is perfectly okay).

3. Using the list above, what do you need in your relationships to feel healthy, encouraged and supported?

4. After spending some time reflecting on this chapter, list any changes you feel intuitively drawn to make regarding support systems. If so, how can you begin making some of these changes?

5. How do you feel about making these changes?

6. How can you practice letting go of fearing changes in relationships? Write a quote or mantra for yourself to be able to look at when you feel the need to control life and relationships.

Chapter 9

Surrendering and Finding Faith

"Faith requires us to believe in something we cannot always rationalize or physically see."

This chapter may be difficult for some of you because of the words I choose to use. Please do not get focused on the words I use to describe my spiritual experiences. Instead focus on big picture. Try to be open to the information and use your words and your beliefs to help you to relate to the content. For example, if my belief is in a Higher Power that I choose to call God and yours is not, then replace the word God with whatever words help you to connect spiritually. For some it is the Universe. For some it is Love. For some it is simply Higher Power. Try to remember, in the grand scheme of things, we all have similar beliefs to describe our spiritual connections. We simply use different words to describe them.

In order to fully heal from my anxiety, depression and eating disorder, I needed to face my hurts from the past and present. I needed to understand my story, feel my feelings, grieve my losses and embrace the changes. I needed to fully break free from my co-dependent ways and I needed to be able to establish healthy boundaries with the people, places and things in my life. I also needed to rebuild my support system by letting go of toxic and unhealthy people who did not support me or allow new people to enter my life. These were not easy tasks for me. In fact, they were ones that required effort and triggered a lot of emotional pain.

I spent most of my life trying to do all of these things my way. I tried to stop binging on my own. I tried to stop purging on my own. I tried to have healthy relationships on my own. I tried to feel happy on my own. I tried to grieve on my own and I tried to make changes on my own. But doing it on my own left me feeling like a failure and brought me right back to square one. In order to fully embrace the changes that were happening in my life, I needed to connect spiritually with a power greater than myself.

My first encounter with God was in private school and Catholic church growing up. I grew up learning many misconceptions about God and was not taught in my religion how to have a relationship with God. I was, however, taught what to do and what not to do to earn His love. As I grew into a young adult I encountered many struggles which led me to explore my faith, my beliefs and my relationship with God. My first real encounter with a loving and forgiving God was in a 12 step program that I attended in my twenties. In program I learned how to admit powerlessness without shame and guilt, how to have faith that God could restore and heal my unhealthy patterns and how to submit and surrender my will to Him by living for His will instead.

Once I began connecting and submitting to God, my life became blessed in more ways than I could ever dream of. I don't know if He blessed me more than before or if I could simply recognize the blessings more. Being able to recognize His work in my life helped me to build my trust and faith in Him.

In order to fully heal from my old, self-destructive ways, I had to fully surrender and become dependent on God, not on other people, places and things. I had to obey His will and plan for my life and leave behind my old patterns and ways. I had to let go of unhealthy people and connect with the ones that He was guiding me to. I needed God to show me how to and where to put up healthy boundaries.

The Stages of Faith-Building

I spent over 15 years trying to figure out how to surrender to God. I could admit my powerlessness over my struggles and I fully believed that God could fix and heal me physically and emotionally, but I could not for the life of me figure out how to let go, submit and surrender my will to Him. I kept trying to control the situations in front of me and would take my will back.

I could not surrender because I did not fully accept God. I did not have faith.

In my mid-thirties, I made the decision to discontinue psychotropic medications I was on for anxiety and depression which resulted in severe withdrawals including insomnia, anxiety and panic for several months. I was faced with one of two options. The first was to go back to using prescription medications to make the symptoms go away and deal with the side effects. The second was to push through the withdrawal and surrender it to God. For the first time in my life I chose to fully surrender to God. In time, the symptoms disappeared and my body re-balanced. I have been med free for 4 years now and have more peace than I ever did in my life.

In order to fully surrender our will and submit to a Higher Power, we need to have faith. Faith comes over time and happens in stages. We go through a series of stages including grief. It's been my experience that we first grieve our expectations of who we think God is or how we think our relationship with Him "should" be. After we fully accept Him, then we build trust in our relationship with Him. This process leads to faith. The following is an explanation of stages we go through while building our faith and trust in God. Included in these stages are thoughts we may have during each stage and prayers to help move through each stage.

1. **Denial and Resistance.** One of the very first stages of faith building is denial and resistance. Half the people I meet with struggle to surrender or let go of a problem because they deny the existence of a Higher Power. They do not understand God and cannot see Him, therefore they do not believe. The other half struggle with resisting the process of surrendering their expectations and will to Him.

While I've always believed in the existence of God, I don't think I fully understood what I was believing in. It wasn't until I began to explore my beliefs that the denial and resistance began to fade. It wasn't until I let go of my understanding of God; who I thought He *should be*, that I was able to see Him in my life. It wasn't until I let go of my expectations of what He *should be* doing in my life and how it *should be* done, that I was able to see Him work in my life.

Even when we believe in God we still struggle with this stage of denial and resistance. Our pride takes over and we think we can do things on our own. We let fear control us and we try to handle a situation on our own. We cannot always see the issue clearly and do not know what needs to be surrendered. We fear what might happen if we allow God to have control and we lack the faith in God needed to fully surrender our problems to Him. We also lack the insight needed to let go of our problems.

We cannot surrender what we cannot see and we cannot see if we do not believe.

• **Thoughts we encounter during this stage:** "God does not exist because if He did, then he would…" "If I let go then……might happen." "What if I let go and He doesn't handle it?" "I don't know how to let go." "I can't see what I need to let go of or how I can let go of it."

- **Pray:** Please remove the blinders from my eyes and help me to see God in my life. Help me to understand what it is that I need to let go of and show me how.

2. **Anger, Blame and Resentment.** During our faith-building journey, we often struggle to understand God's ways. When we begin to have a relationship with God, we start to question why things are the way they are. We question why the world is suffering and why evil things happen. I don't know about you, but for me, the answers to those questions are complicated to understand. Because they are so difficult to process, some of us just avoid thinking about them altogether and don't continue to explore the answers to our questions. Instead we become angry and resentful toward God.

It's easier to be angry with God than to accept that we cannot understand His ways. It is easier to blame God than to look at ourselves and change the things God is showing us needs to be changed. And it is easier be resentful with God than to be patient and wait for answers.

One thing I learned during my faith-building journey is that it is normal to feel angry from time to time in a relationship. I get angry with my husband if I feel that he has done something to hurt me. I get angry with my friend when I don't understand her intentions. Just like those relationships, sometimes I get angry with God when I don't understand what is happening and I cannot see clearly.

Anger can be a normal part of a relationship, especially when we do not understand what is happening. I firmly believe that God understands this. In order to grow in our relationships, we must grieve our perceptions, expectations and disappointments in the relationship; this includes grieving our disappointments and expectations of God. Anger is part of grieving and is therefore a necessary stage in building our faith and trust in God. If we do not acknowledge our anger in relationships, then we learn to mask it and keep it suppressed. Suppressed feelings keep us stuck.

Expectations lead to grief, but faith leads to freedom.

- **Thoughts we encounter during this stage:** Why is God allowing this to happen to me? Why isn't He fixing it? God has abandoned me or won't fix it for me." "If God were fixing my problem, He would be doing it this way…"

- **Pray:** Please be patient with me, forgive me for being angry and grant me peace during this time. Help me to see this situation through Your eyes.

3. **Shame, Guilt and Bargaining.** During this stage of faith building we experience a back and forth conversation in our minds regarding the existence and power God has in our lives. We spend our energy trying to "figure God out" or predict His plans for us. We overanalyze our situations. When things do not go our way, we may experience doubt. We may bargain back and forth between the presence and existence of God. It is a normal, human reaction to question when we do not understand something. But over time, we begin to experience restoration in our situation and therefore begin to feel shame and guilt for ever doubting God.

We all have struggles, no matter how strong our faith is. And we all bargain God's existence and presence in our lives, especially during times of struggle. During my faith-building journey I can remember bargaining a lot. Every time I doubted the existence of God, He would show me otherwise. And every time He showed me otherwise, I felt so ashamed and guilty afterward for ever doubting Him in the first place.

I came to the realization during the bargaining stage that allowing God to work in my life takes time. It takes time because God is not only working in me to change my situation, but He is also working in other people that He uses to change my circumstance. People are not always obedient, therefore, the outcome takes time.

Faith requires us to believe in something we cannot always rationalize or physically see.

- **Thoughts we encounter during this stage:** "Maybe God isn't real." "If God is real, then this wouldn't be happening." "If God is real, then He would answer my prayers." "God answered my prayers in a different way than I expected. I should have never doubted Him." "I've done this before... doubted Him and He has come through."

- **Pray:** Please help me to understand your will in this situation and show me what to do.

4. **Sadness, Loneliness and Depression.** After bargaining back and forth the presence and existence of God in our situation, we begin to experience a sense of deep sadness and loneliness. During this stage we become fully aware of the problem and aware that we do not have control over it. We begin to accept that the situation is not going to change and *we begin to grieve our expectations of God*.

Several years ago I went through a terrible break-up with a very close friend. I was confused and angry and didn't understand why God was allowing this break-up to happen. It didn't make sense to me. It challenged my faith in God more than ever before. I went through isolation from God where I did not reach out and talk to Him about it. When I did start talking to Him, I expressed anger toward Him for allowing it to happen. Once I began to hear Him and see Him at work in the situation, I felt shame and guilt. I bargained His power and existence back and forth upon hearing Him and not hearing Him. Once I became fully convinced of His presence in the situation, I felt an overwhelming sense of sadness and depression. I was able to recognize all the expectations I had of God, which included my expectations of how I believed He should handle the situation. It became clear to me that those expectations kept me from seeing His blessings and work in my life. I cried and grieved those expectations and my relationship with Him shifted completely.

It can be difficult to see God in our lives when we have an expectation of what that might look like.

- **Thoughts we encounter during this stage:** You begin to have more clarity on what it is that you need to accept in a situation and are able to identify the expectations you have of God and how those expectations are keeping you from surrendering the problem to Him. You may say things like, "God's in control." "If it is Your will, then thy will be done." "God knows what is best in this situation." "He has a plan that is far greater than mine."

- **Pray:** Please give me strength and courage to trust and let go of this situation.

5. **Acceptance.** Once we recognize the expectations we have in our relationship with God, we can begin to accept Him for who He is and what He can do. We begin to accept that He is not always going to answer our prayers the way we want and we accept that there is a reason for that. We begin to surrender to Him our problems. This stage will usually involves some kind of break down where we may release words, tears or both. For me, it involved falling to my knees in surrender.

During the acceptance stage of faith-building you accept the situation for being exactly how it is supposed to be. You begin to have a sense of peace and a sense of knowing that God will provide and protect you. You no longer feel fear or insecurity. You no longer analyze your situation or ask the "What ifs."

You no longer battle back and forth in your head. You may even begin to experience and express gratitude for the situation.

Once I was able to recognize that I had expectations of God that were not being fulfilled and surrender those expectations, I was able to accept God's plan for me in the situation. I did not always fully understand His plan or like the way it felt, but I began to trust it. During the acceptance stage I began to see mini miracles and blessings happen as a result of surrendering to Him. The outcome of His way became far greater than what I could do if I had control over the situation. I began to experience gratitude for my pains.

Accepting God comes when we let go of our expectations of Him and replace them with faith in Him.

- **Thoughts we encounter during this stage:** "I can't do this anymore." "Please take control of this situation for me." "I trust that You can and will handle this situation for me."

- **Pray:** Thank you God for this situation and I ask that You not only take it from me, but that You use it for good in my life and others.

6. **Faith Building.** Once we've accepted the situation and have a sense of peace, we can begin to let it go. We begin to move forward fully obeying what God asks of us in the situation without fear. We begin to see positive changes as the result of surrendering our will to God; changes that we can't always make sense of. Our faith begins to grow as we see the outcome of your surrender.

During the faith-building stage we let go of the pain, but may regress back to previous stages in the faith-building process. We experience deeper levels of each stage and can experience them several times. This is because we constantly "take our will back" or try to control the situation again instead of allowing God to have it.

It took me more than half my life to build my full faith in God. Today I can see the events that led to the faith-building stage. I think the faith-building stage lasted the longest for me. I experienced many ups and downs during this stage and regressed back and forth among stages several times. I let go, then took it back, let go, then took it back. Each time I took it back, I experienced grief and each time I let it go, I experienced blessings. The blessings I experienced are what built my faith in God.

Faith in God releases my fears and worries and replaces them with trust and obedience.

- **Thoughts we encounter during this stage:** "I thought I already dealt with this." "I feel like I am right back where I started." "God took care of my last problem, it just took time and patience. Therefore, if I give it time, He will take care of this too."

- **Pray:** Please continue to build my faith and trust in You and help me to see the blessings, both big and small, that you put in front of me.

7. **Trust.** Over time, faith-building turns into complete trust in God where surrendering is not a difficult task anymore, but one that comes almost naturally. In the trust stage, we know that God will provide for us, if we simply let go of trying to control the outcome of the situation. We no longer doubt His promises and we understand that life is full of ups and downs. We understand that difficult times are times where God will grow us and change us for the better. We no longer fear those changes because we know they will make us better people.

Eventually my faith-building ended and I reached a place in my relationship with God where I fully trusted Him in every aspect of my life. I reached a place in my relationship with God where I didn't need anymore reassurance from Him that things were going to turn out okay. I didn't need reassurance that He was real. I understood that His work took time and patience that I lacked and was willing to do the work it took to let go of the situation.

Full trust in God comes only after I am able to surrender my will to Him completely, without needing the reassurance that it will be okay. It is then and only then, that I experience the outcome only He can do.

• **Thoughts we encounter during this stage:** "A problem means that God is working in me and will do something great with me." "This pain means that God is growing me."

• **Pray:** May your will be done, not mine.

The Four Disciplines of Faith-Building

It's been my experience both personally and professionally that surrendering is a process. Much like grief, it is not something that is magical or something that happens overnight. It is something that requires willingness, patience, persistence and prayer.

1. **Willingness.** Often times we have the desire to change something, but we lack the willingness to do what it takes to change. Wanting and being willing are two very different things.

2. **Patience.** In my experience, having the willingness to do something is a process and happens over time so we need to be patient and allow this process to happen in time.

3. **Persistence.** In our society we do not like to or know how to wait for things, therefore, we need to be persistent and not give up. We need to persist in our studies, meditations and prayer time in order to grow in our faith. We will be exploring this more in the next chapter.

4. **Prayer.** It has been my experience that I can be powerless over this process. Often times I lack willingness, patience, and I want to give up. I need God to do what I can't do which is give me the willingness, the patience and the persistence until I am ready to surrender. I ask Him through prayer.

So Now What?

I am hoping you were able to view this chapter with an open mind. No matter what your spiritual beliefs are, chances are you've gone through a similar process or are going through similar stages in your faith-building journey. Keep in mind that faith-building is a process and if you've encountered any of these thoughts, feelings or behaviors, then you are actively seeking God and are right where you need to be. You may be in the beginning stages or you may be in the faith-building stages.

In order to have a relationship with God, we must grieve our expectations. Once we can fully accept God as our Higher Power, that which is beyond what we can comprehend and understand, then we can begin to experience blessings which build our faith. Eventually we learn to trust God with our lives and are able to fully surrender and submit our lives to Him. We no longer need reassurance that He will use our situation to grow us and help others.

Take a moment to reflect on this chapter. Where are you in the faith-building process? Practice self-compassion during the process of faith-building. Do not judge your journey. Be patient with yourself, ask for help and keep your eyes and ears open for His blessings. Do not force anything to happen. Just be.

Questions for Reflection

Find a quiet space where there are little to no distractions. Take a moment in quiet to reflect on what you just read. When you are ready, answer the following questions in your journal.

1. What are your spiritual beliefs or understanding of God? What words do you use to describe God?

2. What expectations do you have of God and how He works in your life?

3. Take a moment to reflect on the "Stages of Faith-Building." Have you experienced any of these stages? Please explain.

4. Where are you now in the "Stages of Faith-Building?" Explain.

5. Do you have any spiritual or religious beliefs, rules or expectations that may be affecting your faith-building process? If yes, then please explain.

6. Of the Four Disciplines of Faith-Building, what discipline or disciplines do you need to have more of in your life? How can you get there?

7. How can you be compassionate with yourself during the faith-building process?

Chapter 10

Prayer, Meditation and Yoga

"By practicing prayer, meditation and incorporating a consistent yoga practice, you will find it faster and easier to ground yourself and keep yourself grounded which means keeping yourself balanced."

We've now uncovered all of the necessary ingredients needed to live a life of balance. We've learned that in order to rebalance our hormones and reduce symptoms of stress, we must live intuitively and practice self-care. Most importantly, we've learned that in order to let go of our past, *live our present intuitively* and work toward our future, we must connect spiritually by connecting intuitively and building a relationship with our Higher Power.

There are many ways to connect to our intuition and maintain a spiritual connection. It's been my experience that the best ways to do this are through prayer, meditation and yoga. Throughout this guide, I've briefly mentioned prayer, meditation and yoga, but I never really explained in detail what each of those are or how to go about doing them.

This chapter is going to explore in depth the importance prayer, meditation and yoga played in my healing process and ways you can incorporate them into your life to help maintain an intuitive living lifestyle.

Prayer

What do you think of when you hear the word prayer? For many, prayer consists of recited words that were learned as a child. Others hear the word prayer and immediately shut down from the idea of praying because it triggers years of religious baggage. But for most, prayer is how we ask God for something when we need it.

To me, prayer is a simple conversation between me and God. As my relationship with God continues to grow, so does my conversation and prayer. I used to recite prayers at night because that is what I was taught as a child. When I went to church, I would recite prayers without understanding the meaning behind them. As a child, I learned that prayer is a way of going to God and requesting something.

As my relationship with God developed and grew stronger, I learned much more about prayer. Prayer is not only about asking God for something, it is also about thanking Him and seeking forgiveness. It is also an opportunity to let go of our problems and turn them over to God. I started practicing this kind of prayer in my mid-thirties and major changes started happening in my life. I'm not sure if the act of prayer actually worked, or if it just helped to ground me each day so that I was better able to recognize the answers I was receiving through prayer. I believe it is a combination of both of those observations.

I've come across many different people from different spiritual walks of life who tell me they are living a spiritual life, but don't know how to pray. The following are tips to help structure your prayer and conversation with God.

1. **Gratitude.** Start your prayer off with gratitude, thanking God for the blessings He's put forth in your life each day. Maybe it is a stranger who gave you a compliment that day. Maybe it is a hug you got from your son or daughter.

Maybe it was the phone call you had with a special person. Practicing gratitude allows us to recognize the good things that God puts in our lives every day.

2. **Forgiveness.** Briefly reflect on anything you are seeking forgiveness for each day. Maybe it is something you said to another person that you are not feeling proud of. Maybe it is the way you talked to yourself that day. Practicing daily repentance frees us from carrying around the burdens and mistakes we hold with us every day and allows us to start with a clean and fresh slate the minute our prayer ends.

3. **Request.** Present your requests to God during your conversation with Him. Let Him know your heart by talking to Him about how you are feeling and what you want Him to help you with. God knows our hearts and knows our minds. God knows our past, present and future. God wants us to seek Him and ask Him for help. He gave us the gift of free will which means that our relationship with Him is a choice. While He knows what we need, He will answer if and only if we ask. Requesting God's help allows our problems to be known to both God and ourselves. It allows God to begin working on our problems.

4. **Accept and let go.** End each prayer asking that God's will be done, not yours. This is an act of turning the problem over, acknowledging that God knows best for your life. It is an act of submitting your will to God's letting go of the outcome. It is an act of surrender and trust.

Meditation

I learned about the benefits of meditation in graduate school. I believe we briefly discussed meditation in one of my classes.

We may have even tried it. Meditation was something we skimmed over, but something that always sparked my attention. Meditation is the act of focusing the brain on the here and now. Meditation was something I was very interested in, but something I could not for the life of me do on my own. I was the queen or racing thoughts and to get my brain to slow down for more than one minute, was impossible.

When I was in my twenties and early thirties, I dabbled in meditation. I maybe made it through a few minutes. Even just a few minutes helped me to feel more peaceful. At the time, I preferred guided meditations where someone talked the entire time in the background. This helped to keep my brain focused.

Meditation has been proven to be just as effective in reducing cortisol levels as an anti-anxiety prescription medication. It is also proven to decrease symptoms of anxiety and depression over periods of time. Meditation is a practice that does not come easy for many. Infact, I've learned that I needed to start with only a few minutes at a time of meditation and build my way up to being able to complete a full class of meditation. Their reason is because the brain is a muscle. Just like going to the gym to grow our muscles, strengthen and condition them, our brains also need to be strengthened and conditioned. Practicing meditation allowed my brain to slowly be able to focus and stop racing. The following is a list of the different kinds of meditation that I've come across during my exploration of meditation.

1. **Guided Meditation.** Guided meditation is practicing meditation with audio or visual in the background. You can attend a meditation class where the instructor will guide you through a specific visualization or mindfulness activity. You can also obtain guided meditations through applications on your phone or computer, podcasts, or Youtube. There are tons of free guided meditations to

choose from.

2. **Movement Meditation.** I find myself most connected and focused when I am engaging in movement. Running and weight lifting is a very meditative activity for me. I experience so much clarity and focus when I am moving. I usually turn on music to help me to focus spiritually.

3. **Musical Meditation.** Music is also where I find that meditative focus and spiritual grounding. Very specific music, such as yoga radio or spa sounds on Pandora, helps me to get focused and meditate.

4. **Quiet Meditation.** Quiet meditation is when there is nothing in the background. One will sit in quiet for minutes at a time and focus the brain on the here and now. I find quiet meditation very powerful, but difficult to do for long periods of time.

Yoga

I had my first experience with the art of yoga in my early twenties. I hated it. I was into running and spinning, not yoga. I hated yoga because it was slow and my brain was not able to slow down enough to focus. I found it excruciating to sit through. I was bored out of my mind. I bought a few home dvd's with good intention to use them. I bought mats and blocks and longed to be a healthy yogi who could meditate and practice yoga every day. I knew it would be good for me and knew it would help me. But still, I could not sit through more than five minutes of yoga without feeling like I was going to crawl out of my skin.

During my mid-thirties, I decided to revisit yoga again. I hadn't been to a yoga class in over 10 years, but I was seeking peace and was desperate to try anything. I attended a class that year that my aunt was assisting at. I LOVED IT!

It was a restorative yoga class that only required me to rest and relax. It included props to help my body to settle into a pose. It included relaxing music, gentle assists and massage. It included meditation. That is my kind of yoga class. The teacher had a soft, eloquent voice and a spoke the words I needed to hear to reground myself. I went back week after week and finally decided to try a retreat at a yoga retreat center in Massachusetts. I continue to attend yoga weekly today and go on retreats twice a year. I still hate certain kinds of yoga, but I found one that I love; one that works for my body and mind.

Just like meditation, if done consistently, yoga is proven to reduce cortisol levels and decrease anxiety and depression. Yoga has so many benefits such as increasing mental focus and clarity and increasing physical flexibility. Yoga is proven to aid in pain relief over time and also reduce tension and headaches. For me, yoga is a place where I can go inward, but I can also connect with God. By slowing down the body and mind, the soul is nourished.

It's been my experience that beginning a yoga practice can be a bit intimidating. There are many unknowns. The following are 4 tips to help begin your yoga practice.

1. **Make the decision to try yoga in a class setting rather than at home.** Life is busy. Whether you are a child, teen or adult, we all have things at home that distract us from staying focused. I tried yoga at home, but the phone would ring, the dryer would stop or there was cleaning to be done. Often times we push things off at home and say we will "do it later". Practicing outside of the home allows for a specific time each week to focus on myself through my yoga practice.

2. **Explore your yoga goals and expectations.** Take some time to research the internet for the different kinds of yoga. Talk

to someone who knows yoga before signing up for a class. Really take the time to think about what you want to accomplish with your yoga practice. Do you want to strengthen your body? Are you looking to quiet the mind? Are you looking to calm your nerves? Are you seeking pain relief? Whatever your goals are, there are lots of options available.

3. **Pick a studio that has a calming atmosphere.** This is very important, especially if you are a sensitive person. Being sensitive can work against you or for you when it comes to yoga. If you are sensitive to sound, touch and sight, you will want to explore what kind of environments are going to calm you and what kinds are going to cause more stress. I went to a yoga class that played soft, calming music, had dim lighting and the teacher provided gentle assists. I loved this class, but parking at the studio was very stressful. I could never find a spot. Once I was able to find a spot, I then had to walk in the dark alone in the city to get to and from the class. I am a country girl, so this was somewhat stressful for me. Whatever stress relief I got from the class was often times compromised by my walk back to my car. I also enjoy lavender oil during yoga class. During certain classes, the instructor will end with a gentle assist or head massage with lavender oil. This is my favorite part of class. Now I seek classes that incorporate this into them.

4. **Shop Around.** Finding a yoga studio, yoga practice and yoga teacher can be similar to finding a therapist or doctor. I often tell clients to shop around until you find the right fit. If you attend a yoga class and do not benefit from it, please understand that it may not be the right kind of yoga for you. My first few experiences with yoga were more exercise based and I did not like them at all. This is why it took me so long to incorporate yoga into my life. I enjoy physical exercise such as spinning and running. It took me years to discover a different form of yoga where you are in resting poses and focusing more on meditation and breathing. I

wish I learned about this kind of yoga years ago. Do not give up until you find what fits your body, mind and spirit.

So Now What?

In a moment you are going to view questions for reflection that will challenge you to explore your practice of prayer, meditation and yoga. While you do not have to try any of these ideas, I highly recommend that you keep an open mind and explore the possibility of trying them and adding them into your self-care practice. By practicing prayer, meditation and incorporating a consistent yoga practice, you will find it faster and easier to ground yourself and keep yourself grounded which means keeping yourself balanced. Do not try to adopt someone else's ideas of prayer, yoga and meditation. Instead, explore these practices on your own and listen to your intuition regarding what practices are best for you. And lastly, have fun! My hope is that you will listen to your body, mind and spirit and find a practice that allows you to connect to your inner self and your Higher Power, opening doors and opportunities for spiritual wisdom and growth.

Questions for Reflection

Find a quiet space where there are little to no distractions. Take a moment in quiet to reflect on what you just read. When you are ready, answer the following questions in your journal.

1. Since you've started your intuitive living journey, have you started any practices of prayer, meditation or yoga? If so, has it helped you and how (be as specific as you can)?

2. If you were to begin a prayer regimen, what might it look like?

3. If you were to begin a meditation regimen, what might it look like?

4. If you were to begin a yoga regimen, what might it look like?

5. Do you have any fears or inner critic judgments about exploring prayer? Meditation? Yoga? If so, what are they and what might help to overcome each of them?

6. Take some time this month to explore three new things mentioned in this article. Maybe it will be prayer or a new yoga class. Maybe it will be to sign up for a beginner's meditation class or workshop. Keep in mind that walking out in nature can be considered a meditative practice. Listening to spiritual music can be meditative. Maybe you are looking to explore new movement activities. There is a whole world of spiritual practice out there that is proven to promote mindfulness and healing. After you've experienced each new thing, write about your experience, both good or bad.

Chapter 11

Giving and Receiving Grace

"Grace allows me to live my life with purpose instead of living my life in emotional bondage and captivity to self and others."

What do you think of when you hear the word grace? To me grace is the act of loving without judgement or expectation; it is allowing another person to be who they are regardless of who I think they should or should not be and what I think they deserve or don't deserve. A person can give grace to another human being and they can receive grace from another human being. When I think of giving and receiving grace, I think of giving and receiving unconditional love, acceptance and forgiveness. Grace is not earned or deserved, it just is.

In 2014 I experienced a tremendous loss and rejection. Out of nowhere, I was dumped by my best friend. I talked about this experience in the prologue of this book. We were very close friends for years and years. Our husbands were close. Our children were close. She was going through some trouble emotionally and one day decided that she no longer wanted to be friends. She could not give me a reason, she just picked up and abandoned the friendship.

The pain I felt during this loss was probably the most pain I'd ever experienced. I had no closure from the relationship. I felt ashamed for many reasons, as there was blame she put on me for the reason why the relationship did not work. The worst part of all was that they lived three houses down from us. So, day after day, I was reminded of the pain. I would drive by and my heart would ache. It took me over two years to fully grieve that relationship. I was stuck in the grief for two whole years, struggling to let go of the pain, the anger, the guilt, the shame and sadness.

About one year into the relationship, learned about grace during a small group study. I was encouraged to pray for this friend and her family. Mustering up the strength to pray for someone who hurt you or whom you are angry and resentful toward is not an easy thing to do. But I was desperate to feel better and willing to do anything to make the pain go away. I was told that if I prayed for her, then the anger and feelings I had toward her would disappear.

To be honest, I did not start praying for her to help her. I started praying for her to help me. I prayed to God asking Him to bless my friend and also asking Him to help me to forgive her. And about a year and a half into my grief, I was able to forgive her for abandoning our friendship. I was able to let go without understanding why she left. I was able to let go without knowing if she would ever come back. A few months later I received a message from her. She asked to get together. We met and she asked me for forgiveness for the pain she caused me and my family. Immediately I gave it to her and told her that I had forgiven her a long time ago. She did not understand the grace she'd received from me, but accepted it.

Today, our relationship is extremely distant. I have forgiven the hurt, but unfortunately one does not forget the pain and today I struggle to fully engage myself in the relationship without specific reciprocations and boundaries in place. Unfortunately those reciprocations are not happening, so the boundaries are in place. But the pain does not control my life anymore. It does not rob me of my joy. It is just there in the back as a memory. Because of my extension of grace, was I able to let go and move through my grief.

This is only one of several examples that I could share. I spent so much of my life holding onto anger and shame. Anger and shame distracted me and kept me from being the person I was created to be. Just imagine how life would be different if we lived with grace; loving everyone around us unconditionally, regardless of who they are and what they've done. Imagine if we extended more grace toward ourselves.

Grace is not something that comes easy to human beings. In order to give and receive grace, we must be able to let go of our expectations of ourselves and others and practice accepting life as being exactly how it is in the present moment. We must learn to see ourselves and others through spiritual eyes rather our own.

Expectations and Grace

My first step in being able to give and receive grace, was being able to identify the expectations I had of myself and others. This meant also identifying and acknowledging where those expectations came from.

Let me take you back to our earlier chapter on expectations. We learn what we live. We live what we learn. That means our family environment, our society, our culture and our religious and spiritual beliefs all play part in our expectations of self and others.

I grew up in a critical environment. Whether it be in my family, my social circles, my culture or my religion; shame, judgement and criticism were the key ingredients in that shaped my view of myself and others. The culture in my family was one with strong opinions and judgement of others. I grew up in a small town and was sheltered from a lot of hardship that you would find if you grew up in the city. This skewed my view of people and left me ignorant in so many ways. My religious beliefs were punitive, shameful and judgmental as well. Grace was definitely something I learned later in life.

My education in psychology and social work made me a more analytical and judgmental person. Instead of judging others on my standard, I was also judging them according to the DSM. I was trained to recognize what is considered healthy and what is not. I was trained to recognize dysfunction. I literally made a career out of judging people on what is and is not considered normal. I made a career of telling people what is wrong with them.

In a clinical setting, this was not a big deal. I had boundaries to protect me from being hurt by others. I was the counselor and they were the client; therefore I was the one diagnosing and they were the one being diagnosed. My emotions were detached with regard to how I felt about them as a person in a relationship with me; therefore, who they were and what behaviors they displayed in relationships did not trigger me. But I carried my work into my personal life and began diagnosing the people and the world around me. Everywhere I went, I was able to identify dysfunction. Why? Because we live in a broken world with extremely broken people. But instead of feeling sorry for them, I became triggered and angry.

I took their brokenness personally. Instead of acknowledging that people are broken, I internalized their behaviors and projected them onto myself. I did this because deep inside I did not feel good enough, so I assumed that the world felt that way about me too. In no time, I was a bitter and angry person who lacked the ability to give and receive grace because I didn't know what grace was.

Instead of forgiving others and letting go of hurts, I held onto them. I clutched them as tight as I could and I lived my life obsessing about all the things people did wrong; especially my own wrongs. It wasn't until I learned about grace that I was able to see people through different eyes. Once I could see through eyes of grace, I was able to show compassion to both myself and others; freeing myself from the years of bondage to self and uncovering a person who was full of life, encouragement and purpose.

Grief and Grace

Acceptance is a key term we've discussed throughout this book. Acceptance is the act of surrendering our expectations of ourselves and others. I've shared my struggles with acceptance; my struggles to accept others for exactly how they are and also my struggles to accept myself for how I am. I used to get stuck in grief which affected me in so many negative ways. I lived life feeling angry and irritable with almost everyone; especially myself. Nobody could live up to my standard of perfection. In turn, I had few close friendships. I wore a mask most days, pretending I liked the people I was hanging around with, only to go home and talk incessantly about them regarding how I felt that they had wronged me; how I felt that they did not deserve my love or friendship.

Sometimes they did wrong me, but I carried that anger around for years and years. I was unable to let it go which kept me from being able to enjoy life. It kept me from being able to acknowledge gratitude. It kept me stuck in grief going back and forth between anger, guilt and shame. Because of the way I viewed people and their behaviors, I became toxic not only to myself, but I also became toxic to those around me; radiating negativity wherever I went. I was stuck in the pit of my own grief.

I grew up with a perfectionist personality. I had high standards of both myself and others. My mind saw life one way and it was either black or white. This means I saw myself one way; either good or bad. Most of the time I could not live up to my own expectations of self. So I learned to view myself as bad.

In no time I began punishing myself with negative messages. I used food to cope with how I felt about myself and the more I ate, the more I hated myself. My eating disorder became the biggest cycle of disgrace I could have toward myself.

Receiving Grace

In my thirties I started attending a non-denominational church in the city where I learned about grace. I learned that the word grace is about loving, accepting and forgiving unconditionally. Beyond that, grace is about being loved, accepted and forgiven without having to do something to earn it. I am given grace simply because I am me.

Have you ever done something you were not proud of? I think most of us can answer yes to this question. There are many parts of who I am today that I am still not proud of; parts I pray for God to change to make me a better version of who He created me to be. Those parts of me that I am not proud of include ego and pride. I am able to recognize those traits in me and they are ugly; they trigger feelings of shame. My old way of dealing with those traits was to mask them and hide them; cover them up so they looked good so that nobody would know. I would lie about them and deny them. I would defend them and resist them.

All of these actions only kept me from working through them; from embracing them, accepting them and letting them go. The perfectionist in me could not bear to look at the parts of me that I do not like. The perfectionist in me could not bare to have those parts exposed to those around me, because if they were exposed, then people might not like me. And if people realized who I really was, then they might reject me.

This cycle of denial and resistance; this cycle of shame, kept me in bondage to self. It kept me trapped in lies and trapped in a mask that I could not for the life of me take off. Looking back, I carried that shame around and wore that mask because I feared the exposure. In my past experiences, exposure led to rejection. Rejection led to pain.

At age thirty-five I became so desperate to heal from my anxiety, depression and eating disorder that I decided to take the mask off and reveal the parts of me that I did not like. What I discovered was an indescribable grace that was given to me; a kind of grace that allowed me to poke through the thick denial I had built up. Little by little, parts of me were exposed and people did not run. I allowed God to grant me grace and then allowed myself to do the same. After practicing receiving grace in the privacy of my relationship with God, I began to branch out and share more with the people God put in my life. This included my church family at first. Most of them gave me that same grace that God was giving me. The shame slowly melted away and I began to heal.

Ways to Receive Grace

Because I allowed myself to receive grace, I am now able to recognize the purpose in what used to cause me so much shame and pain. Receiving grace is a necessary step in being fully renewed. The following are ways we can receive grace:

1. **Be real with God.** In Catholic church I was taught to fear God. I was taught to hide from Him. I was taught to earn His love and to repent if I did something "bad." Does this sound like a relationship you want to be honest in? My answer was "No way!" As my spiritual life began to heal,

my relationship with God grew stronger. I began to talk with Him about everything. I began to share the deepest and darkest, most shameful parts of myself. By opening up to God and having an honest conversation with Him about my struggles, I was able to receive His grace. I could not receive His grace when I was living behind a mask of lies.

2. **Allow yourself to be real and vulnerable with others.** Opening up to others was really hard for me. I struggled with communication. I could not effectively express myself with words; therefore, I kept quiet. I wore my mask and acted as the counselor who had no problems. I eventually found a place where I felt safe enough to begin to say aloud my struggles. Little by little I opened up and became vulnerable. I learned that most people appreciated the vulnerability and in turn either gave me feedback and encouragement or opened up about something similar they were struggling with. Vulnerability in relationships allowed for me to receive grace from others. And if others could give me grace, then I could give myself grace.

3. **Allow yourself to be forgiven.** I think I held onto shame without knowing it. I had trouble letting go of it. But once I learned to receive forgiveness from God and others, I quickly learned that I could forgive myself. Forgiveness is an act of grace.

4. **Accept love from others.** People show love in many ways. Some show love through touch, some through giving, some with words, some with being present, and some by doing. I had trouble receiving all of the above. I had to be mindful with this practice of receiving in order for it to become more comfortable for me to receive, especially when I felt like it was undeserved.

5. **Say thank you.** The act of gratitude is not only polite, but it is also a way of accepting and receiving. You may not always like what you are receiving or understand why you

are receiving it, but practice saying thank you anyway. Gratitude is an act of humility, which is an act of grace.

6. **Look people in the eyes.** You cannot receive anything if you do not look people in the eyes. Looking someone in the eyes allows them to connect with you. If you always walk around afraid to look at people, you will never fully connect with anyone.

7. **Be present.** Stop talking, stop fixing, stop fighting, and stop hiding. Try just being present in the moment with another human being. Sometimes, we spend so much energy doing things that we miss the opportunities and graces that come to us by simply being present. There are times when it is completely appropriate to show up and just be present.

Giving Grace

Giving grace to someone does not mean that I allow them to treat me poorly, abuse me or take advantage of me. It means that I am able to view them through a different lens and forgive them. It means that I can still love them and not always like them. Grace allows me to let go of the hurts that people cause me because they are people and they are human. Grace allows me to show love to all people, just different kinds of love with different kinds of people. Most of all, grace allows me to be an encourager instead of discourager.

The following are ways we can give grace to others, including ourselves.

1. **Kind words.** I used to live with a chip on my shoulder. Because of that, sometimes the words that came out of my mouth were not kind. Today, I still have days where my mouth gets the best of me. Kind words go a long way. Remember, grace is not about what is earned or deserved. Grace is just because. Use kind words.

2. **Smile.** I live in New England. One of the biggest jokes around here is that we New Englanders don't smile. It is so true! Years ago I started walking around like "Buddy the Elf" and started smiling at everyone I walked passed. Smiling is an act of grace. It changes the energy in the environment. Again, I don't pick and choose who to smile to based on whether they deserve it or not. I just smile and say hello or good morning or good afternoon. Then, I carry on with my business. SMILE!

3. **Small gestures.** This can be a challenge, especially if you hold resentment toward a person. But the whole point of learning grace is to learn how to let go of that resentment. Doing small, kind gestures for a person you may be struggling to get along with is a great way to extend grace to someone. Very often, after you do those gestures, you are blessed with peace.

4. **Forgive.** This is another tough one for many, especially if you are holding on to resentment or have an opinion about what a person has done. That break-up with my friend a few years ago was probably the hardest loss I'd ever been hit with. The two years of grieving was a heavy grief and I lost so much during that extended period of time. Into the second year, I started practicing forgiveness. I would say it out loud. At first I did not mean it, but eventually, the forgiveness came. I still didn't understand my friend's reasons for leaving and I still don't, but I was able to forgive her anyway because of grace. She didn't deserve the forgiveness at all, but I still gave it to her. She didn't ask for it, but I still gave it to her. And something inside of me was healed because of that. The anger faded and the sadness melted. Forgiveness brought me the peace I was longing for and helped me to move on.

5. **Show gratitude.** You don't have to understand or agree with the opinions, judgements or behaviors of others, but you can still respond in a way that gives grace. I have a family member that I have a really hard time getting along with. It is hard to talk to this person. It is hard to say kind words and it is hard to smile around him. He has done some pretty mean things to my family. For years I held onto the judgement and anger. But I learned to accept him for who he is in the present moment. I do not hang out with this person, but I do use kind words when I see him. I show gratitude when I go to his home. I say hello and thank you. It can be that simple. A year ago, he lashed out and passed some judgements onto me in anger. Instead of getting defensive and fighting back like I used to do, I said, "Thank you for your perspective on that. I will think about that." I walked away and left the event we were at because I did not feel comfortable being there. I honored myself, but I was able to give grace through gratitude to someone whom I did not agree with or like at the moment.

6. **Be present.** Again, stop talking, fixing, fighting or hiding. Just show up and be present. You cannot extend grace to someone if you are talking at them, trying to fix them, fighting with them or hiding from them. Sometimes, our bodies need to just be present to allow the grace to flow out of us onto another person. Sometimes our presence says it all.

7. **Keep your opinions and judgements to yourself.** I AM NOT ALWAYS GOOD AT THIS ONE! I like to give my input as much as I can, but I am learning that unless someone asks my opinion, it's not mine to give. Extend grace, by keeping your thoughts to yourself, unless of course, the person asks for your opinion.

So Now What?

Try applying this concept of grace to your life. Where do you need more grace? Is it with yourself or with someone else? Think about what the world would be like if we lived a life with more grace.

Take a moment to reflect on what is holding you back from being able to give and receive grace in your life. Is it the expectations you have of yourself and others? Is it the act of accepting people and letting go of those expectations and beliefs? Prayerfully reflect today asking God to reveal truth to you with regard to your ability to give and receive grace. Having awareness is the first step in being able to overcome our struggles. Practice self-compassion by allowing truth to come to light without shame or judgement; thereby practicing grace with ourselves.

And lastly, allow yourself to see people through spiritual eyes, not sensitive eyes. Spiritual eyes are eyes of love; eyes of peace. Spiritual eyes free us from bondage to self. Spiritual eyes free us from judgement and shame. Spiritual eyes allow us to understand that people are human and don't always see the world the way we are seeing it. Make a note of how this changes how you view yourself and others.

Questions for Reflection

Find a quiet space where there are little to no distractions. Take a moment in quiet to reflect on what you just read. When you are ready, answer the following questions in your journal.

1. What would your world look like if there was more grace in it?

2. In what areas of your life do you need more grace? Is it with yourself or with another person?

3. What is holding you back from giving or receiving grace?

4. Does grief (the inability to let go of expectations and accept a person, place or thing) impact your ability to give or receive grace? Explain.

5. Using the list above, what are some ways you can begin to receive grace from God or others?

6. Using the list above, what are some ways you can extend grace to others today?

7. Write a prayer that you can pray, asking your Higher Power to help you with this idea of grace.

Chapter 12

Finding Purpose and Taking Risks

"True happiness comes from the blessings we receive when we live out our life purpose."

I see many different kinds of people, struggling with many different problems in life. During their initial visit with me, they are asked to fill out an intake form. The last question they are asked on the form is, "What are your long-term goals for therapy or coaching?" Ninety-nine percent of my clients answer the same thing, "To feel happy and to not struggle anymore." During our discussion, I ask them what they think will make them happy. Again, the answers are always similar and include people, places and things that fill an expectation of peace, joy and fulfillment. You know, the "if only's". "If only my husband were more loving." "If only I was thinner." "If only my children helped out." "If only my family got along." "If only my boss wasn't such a jerk". You see, we live our lives seeking a feeling of happiness and contentment. We believe that if only (insert word here) were different, then I would be happy.

We live our lives either fighting for happiness or avoiding the pain of failed expectations; therefore we live our lives in survival. Living in a constant state of fight or flight is living in a constant state of stress.

Life is crazy! Let's just face the hard core facts right now. We are living to survive this messed up, crazy world. We spend much energy trying to survive that we end up missing the meaning and purpose of our existence. We struggle simply because our long term goal is to find happiness. We don't understand that happiness is a feeling and feelings come and go. Just like struggle, happiness will pass too. It is impossible to live happy and peaceful all of the time; therefore, living to find happiness just does not work. And if we live our lives expecting and seeking happiness all the time, then we are living to survive this messed up world. Do you see the cycle we create?

I used to live my life this way. I thought the purpose of life was to find happiness and avoid pain. This meant seeking people, places and things that brought me joy and breaking free from people, places and things that caused me pain. My goals in life were to find a job that made me happy, to make the amount of money that made me happy, to meet the right people that made me happy, to have children that made me happy, and to look a certain way so that I would feel happy about myself. Don't get me wrong, those things all made me very happy. And there is nothing at all wrong with wanting those things. But what I discovered was that those things either do not last or they let me down. The things I thought made me happy only brought short-term happiness because the excitement in those things would fade. I lived my life battling the ups and downs; constantly seeking happiness and never embracing the purpose or meaning of my life.

I had an expectation of what my life needed to look and feel like in order to be happy. The kind of happiness I was seeking was the result of what I could get or what I could achieve. It was all about me. And in order to find true balance and fulfillment, I had to grieve that expectation and learn a new way of thinking about the purpose and meaning of life. I had to learn how to live with a different intention; an intention to give of myself instead of the intention of living to get for myself. It was then that I learned how to live my purpose. And I know that if you live your life with the kind of intention I'm about to teach you, then you will be blessed with more joy and happiness than you could ever imagine. You see, the happiness we all seek is the result of living our life purpose.

Purpose

Take a moment to reflect on your life. What are you living your life for? Are you living your life like most people, constantly in survival mode and desperately trying to seek happiness or avoid struggles? What are your expectations of happiness?

I'm going to challenge you to think about the purpose and meaning of life in a way that may be a bit different from how you've thought about it before. I don't have some wacky intention of trying to manipulate your thinking or change your beliefs. I'm simply sharing my understanding of what our human existence is all about. Why? Because my understanding works! It allowed me to shift from living for myself, which got me nowhere, to living with intention and meaning, which changed my whole perspective.

It's been my experience that we have three basic life purposes: a universal purpose, a communal purpose and personal purpose. In grade school we were taught story writing using the 5 W's and 1 H, who, when, where, what, why and how. I'm going to break these three purposes down into very simple terms for you to understand using the 5 W's and 1 H to help you write YOUR STORY.

1. **Universal Purpose.** A universal purpose answers the question "what and why" with regard to the purpose of our human existence. There is one universal answer to that question and it applies to all human beings. *Our universal purpose is to matter.* Why matter? Because your life impacts how another person matters and their life impacts another and so on. Your universal purpose is the same as my universal purpose.

2. **Communal Purpose.** A communal purpose answers the questions "who, when, and where" with regard to the purpose of our human existence. Who are you called to matter to? When are you called to matter to them? And where are you called to matter? Your communal purpose evolves over time and is always changing. My communal purpose during childhood (the when) was to matter to the people in my family, in the schools I went to and the town I lived in (the who and the where). It changed as I grew older and had a family of my own. It changes with every season of life and if I allow it to happen intuitively it brings peace.

3. **Personal Purpose.** A personal purpose answers the question "how" with regard to the purpose of our human existence. How you matter is by using the spiritual gifts you were born with. We all have spiritual gifts. Some are very simple gifts and some are a bit more complex. But all gifts matter and are necessary in the existence of human life. Your personal purpose is going to be different from mine because it is based off of your gifts and talents. You see, we all matter in this world. What you do, where you do it, how you do it, when you do it, why you do it and who you do it to or with, matters. I heard this analogy in a movie called, "We Believe" that talks about each life representing a thread being sewn into a large quilt. It has a unique color, shape and size that adds to the quilt. Your life, or piece of thread, weaves over and under other threads making a beautiful creation. Your piece of thread is necessary to make the creation complete. Your life matters to every person, place and thing you come into contact with. Last week I found a short story written by my 9 year old son. It was a story about the day we went to the airport to pick up our new puppy, Bauer. I was a bit nervous that day as I never ordered a puppy online and didn't know what to expect when we got to the airport. My son wrote a detailed story that described our interactions with him that evening. His memory of who was present, where we were, how we

spoke to him, what we said to him, how we comforted him or did not comfort him were so vivid. As I read the story I was so thankful that from his perspective I was kind and loving to him during that experience. The reality is that I was completely stressed out and could have been snippy. Reading that story made me realize that my life and how I behave really matters to his life. That memory was a very positive memory for my son, but it could have been a negative one.

Ways to Uncover Your Life Purpose

I see so many people who struggle to find their life purpose. As I stated above, we all have the same universal purpose, but our communal and personal purpose is different. They are based on our gifts and talents, but they are also based on our experiences in life, which include our struggles and shortcomings. The following are ways to uncover your life purpose.

1. **Practice Self-Care.** Our purpose in life evolves and changes over time, so it is important that we practice being present, connected and balanced so we can see and hear God's vision and plan for us. Practicing self-care on a regular basis fosters balance and keeps the mind, body, and spirit open and ready to receive guidance from your intuition.

2. **Pray.** Prayer is our way of communicating with God. This includes asking Him for help and guidance. When I am struggling to find fulfillment or purpose in my life, I pray. I ask God to show me what He wants of me, how He wants me to do it and I ask for Him to bless me with the time, energy and resources to carry it out. Prayer is a necessary action I must take in order to uncover my purpose. Without asking for guidance, I am left to my own will.

3. **Listen.** After prayerfully asking for God to use me, show me and bless me with what I need to uncover and live out my purpose, I must take the time to listen to what He is telling me. Often times we take the time to ask God for help, but we have an expectation of what the outcomes are supposed to look like, therefore, we completely miss the answers He gives us. God will reveal Himself through your thoughts in your mind, through others in your life or simply in something you see or read on the side of the road. Keep your eyes and ears open and take the time to sit in quiet and just listen.

4. **Obey.** Once receiving answers from God, we must obey what He tells us to do. This is often times the hard part; the part that most people procrastinate about due to fear and doubt. This is where we must submit to God and do His will, not ours, trusting that His will is better for us.

Challenges You May Face

Uncovering your purpose is not always easy to do. It can be a process and requires much work and energy. The following are some challenges you may face while uncovering your purposes in life.

1. **Requires us to be aware and work through our struggles.** As discussed in previous chapters, in order to make any kind of change, we must first have awareness of what needs to be changed. Many people struggle and are challenged to find purpose because of our natural instinct to deny and resist a problem; fight or flight change.

2. **Requires us to make time for self-care.** In order to maintain presence and awareness, we must practice being balanced so we can be open to receiving that awareness. We do this by practicing self-care. But practicing self-care and maintaining that balance requires us to make time for things

such as prayer, meditation and yoga, etc. Many of us struggle and resist making our self-care a priority until we are desperate for the changes.

3. **Requires you to take a risk.** Our purpose may require us to take risks and do things that make us feel uncomfortable. An example is writing this book. I am petrified of what you will think of me. I am petrified that the thoughts I put down on paper will be challenged, judged and criticized. I am petrified that you will think it is stupid. I am petrified to get a bad review. I am petrified of my family and friends reading it and being angry with me. I am petrified of hurting my parents. I am petrified of my church reading it and not agreeing with the terminology I use to describe my spiritual experiences. I am scared of so many things, but I am taking that risk because I feel God telling me to do it. God is first in my life, not my family, friends, parents or church, husband or children. Submitting to God can be risky and we may lose things. But I can assure you that He knows and will replace those losses with blessings.

4. **You may go off the path from time to time by taking risks.** We are not perfect; therefore, we will not do our purpose perfectly. Sometimes I think God is speaking to me and telling me to do something, but later I learn that I was practicing my will, not His. But one thing I learned during my faith-building stage is that, no matter what I do, even if I make a mistake, God can and will fix it. Again, He knows my heart and He knows that I am not perfect. He is my guide and He fixes my mistakes and puts me right back on the correct path. You cannot be afraid to make a mistake because mistakes will happen when you are practicing intuitive living, especially when you are practicing obedience. But it's okay because God's got this!

5. **Goes against the norm.** Another challenge is breaking social rules and norms. Often times, God will ask you to do something that requires you to go against a social rule or norm. The challenge becomes the people around you and how they respond to your obedience. Some may appreciate and like it and some may hate it. You may experience rejection and hurt from others as a result of your obedience, but rest assured that it is not a punishment. Rejection is a reflection of what is going on in their life and has nothing to do with you.

6. **Challenges Inner Critic.** The fear of being wrong and making a mistake can be a big challenge because it triggers the inner critic. The inner critic can really keep us stuck and deter us from being obedient to our purpose. And because our inner critic gets triggered, our stress gets triggered and we are more likely to resist or deny; fight or flight.

7. **Things may get harder before they get easier.** It has often been my experience when making changes in my life, taking risks and obeying God, that things sometimes blow up and get worse before they get better. This is exactly why people do not submit and obey God's will for them. They learn to shut Him out and not listen. They learn to fight or flight and it becomes a habit. They learn to live in denial and resistance. Why? Because obeying God triggers fear and discomfort. Often times the culture around us or the dynamics in the circles of people that surround us, fall apart when we make a changes. The people in our lives become uneasy and because we change something, it forces a domino effect and they are then forced to do something different. PEOPLE DO NOT LIKE CHANGE; therefore, they may become resistant to our changes and things may get harder for a while. But eventually, they will calm down and those around us get used to the changes.

So Now What?

You are here on this earth, living this life for a reason and that reason is to matter. This is not a religious belief, it is a spiritual truth. And I am telling you, if you practice all of the things we talked about in this book so far, then you too will begin to hear God speak purpose, plan and vision into your life. And if you obey what He is telling you to do, then you will be blessed with so much more than you could ever dream of or imagine. Start by asking God what His plans are for your life, then take some time to listen and hear how He is telling you to accomplish them. Submit and obey and see where He will take you and how He will bless you.

Questions for Reflection

Find a quiet space where there are little to no distractions. Take a moment in quiet to reflect on what you just read. When you are ready, answer the following questions in your journal.

1. Do you live your life with purpose, meaning and intention or do you live your life in survival? Explain.

2. If your universal life purpose is to matter, then where or how are you doing this in your life? Explain.

3. What community of people are you called to matter to? How are you called to do this?

4. What are the gifts, talents and skills that you were blessed with? Do you use them with intention and purpose? Please explain. If you answered no, then why not?

5. What are or have been your personal life experiences, including struggles? Do you share them with intention and purpose? Please explain. If you answered no, then why not?

6. Using the list of "Ways to Uncover Your Purpose," what are some ways you are willing to uncover your life purpose?

7. Using the list of "Challenges You May Face" in this chapter, what are some challenges you've faced with trying to live with intention and purpose? Add to the list in this chapter if you can.

Chapter 13

Pride to Humility

"A prideful person sees through a human lens, but a humble person sees through a spiritual lens."

One of the biggest things I struggled with in life and continue to struggle with is relationships. I am a very aware person who was trained to analyze my world. I grew up being critical and judgmental of both myself and others. I was extremely insecure with myself; how I looked and how others perceived me. My inner critic controlled my thoughts. I left social situations obsessing about the interactions that occurred and beating myself up for saying or not saying things I believed I should have or should not have said. It felt like everyone had an ulterior motive, which was to hurt me and I just couldn't seem to get past the negative thinking. I created stories in my mind that projected a negative outcome and I could only see that outcome. As a result, I was a bitter, resentful and angry person in relationships. My anger affected my relationship with my family, my relationship with my husband, my relationship with friends and my relationship with myself. A few years ago I began to recognize that my issue was not the result of other people's behavior or due to a low self-esteem. My issue was pride.

My biggest lesson in pride has come through the lessons I've learned fighting and advocating for the needs of my children in a public school. Three years ago, while my daughter was in second grade, I met with her teacher to discuss concerns I had regarding my daughter's progress at school. I was concerned specifically with her reading and comprehension. Her teacher told me that she was just insecure and needed a lot of reassurance, which affected her scores in the classroom. I told the teacher that I disagreed, but because I was a people pleaser I stepped down from arguing and allowed my daughter to be pushed up to third grade. My daughter continued to struggle through the beginning of third grade with reading, spelling, organization, understanding directions and short term memory. Being a counselor who sees multiple kids with learning disabilities, I knew something was wrong. I called a school meeting and pushed for academic testing to be done. I was angry and resentful at the time because nobody was listening to my concerns and instead they kept telling me she was just insecure and anxious. After much pleading, the special education team agreed to test her. The testing showed NOTHING!

At the time I was questioning a central processing disorder, so I also had her tested by an audiologist outside of school. Her results showed significant issues with processing. Feeling validated, I presented the results to the school and my daughter received some accommodations, but no extra help academically. Her anxiety got worse as she struggled to complete classwork and assignments.

I was angry that the school would not give her special education and I tried desperately to understand why. As I got and angrier, I began lashing out through emails to her teachers and guidance counselors. Every time I saw her struggle, I knew there was something more wrong, but they brushed me off when I brought it up.

In 2015 I hit a breaking point after learning that her 4th grade teacher was not following her accommodations at school. After giving the teacher and the school the benefit of the doubt for 2 years, I called another meeting. Because I was angry and felt somewhat validated by her central processing results, I was a bit more assertive at this meeting and told them that their lack of follow through was unacceptable. Some of them agreed and immediately began putting more accommodations into place. None of the accommodations helped her learning struggles. I had her retested by her audiologist and it was confirmed that she was still struggling. That summer her report card came home with below grade level scores in reading and writing. I finally had enough information to prove to her school that her disability was impacting her academic performance.

I prayed to God for three years regarding my daughter's educational needs. I prayed for Him to put the right person on my daughter's path that would understand her disability, be able to recognize her deficits and advocate for her educational needs. Instead of accepting defeat, I continued to battle the school, determined to prove that I was right. Instead of stepping back and getting a tutor outside of school or paying for private school, I continued to put both myself and my daughter through stress because I needed to prove my point.

We met this past summer and had a very lengthy meeting. I remained calm, but assertive, through the entire meeting. They finally agreed that they would retest her, but asked that we wait until the start of the school year. They told me that we would be meeting the first week of school with the intention to sign the paperwork necessary to have her tested. I could have signed it in that moment, but I agreed to wait to allow both my daughter and the teachers the rest of their summer without testing. I thanked God for opening their eyes and hearts to be able to hear me and listen to me.

We met at the start of the school year as discussed to sign the paperwork. Only instead of signing the paperwork, they spent the meeting re-discussing whether or not we should test my daughter. I was so angry. The end result of that meeting was defeat once again. They bullied me into waiting another eight weeks and stated that they wanted to see what the teacher thought AGAIN!

After that meeting I let go of putting my faith in the educational staff. And as much as it pained me, I made a decision that I would pay the money to have her privately tested at Boston Children's Hospital. I made the call to put her on the waiting list for testing and I started looking into outside tutoring and private schools that I really did not want to spend my money on. I battled that voice in my head that reminded me that my daughter "deserved" extra help at the school and that we pay our taxes for an adequate education. I surrendered my pride and humbly admitted defeat.

A few weeks after humbly admitting defeat, I received a call from a Special Education Teacher from my daughter's school. She requested to have my daughter tested immediately. She said that she could see a mild disability and wanted to get her on an IEP as soon as possible. I cried tears of joy. My fight was over and my daughter would finally receive the help she needed. And I gained a lesson in humility.

This is just one of many struggles I've encountered in the public education system with my children. You see, I spent years holding onto anger and resentment with regard to my children's' educational needs. That anger consumed me at times and held me captive, keeping me from living a life of health, balance and purpose. I had to let go of my pride; knowing that I was right and that we were not getting the services or education my daughter "deserved" and that our tax dollars were paying for. I was right in the end, but it is only through humility that her needs are being met. It is by letting go and surrendering the outcome that her needs are being met, not by being right or winning the battle. Most importantly, it is through humility that I was able regain peace and find a healthy balance of mind, body and spirit.

Pride

I always thought pride meant being arrogant, selfish, thinking of oneself as being better or more important than others and not being able to admit when wrong. Pride is certainly all of those things, but it is much more than that. A few years ago I began to study pride and I realized that being prideful can also include our negative perception of self. By saying we are not good enough, we are saying that God made a mistake with us. By saying we can't do something we are saying that we are in control of our lives; we are more powerful and know more than God. By saying we are not worthy or by being self-consumed in our own appearance, gifts and talents we are saying that those things are more important than God's purpose for putting us here on earth. While researching the word pride, I came across the following characteristics:

- Having an inflated sense of self or thinking that you are better than others.
- Arrogance and selfishness.
- Being defensive.
- Not taking responsibility or ownership.
- Inability to listen to another person's point of view is the same as saying that your way is the only way.
- Being fearful or anxious is the result of not trusting God. Distrust in God represents a belief that you know more than God.
- Controlling people, places and things is an inability to surrender which is another form of distrust in God's will and plan for your life.
- Having a deserving attitude.
- Someone who is negative all the time and can only see the bad in things.
- Someone who has expectations of perfection.
- Consumed with what others think of them.
- Judgmental and critical of others.
- Breaks rules and doesn't follow directions.
- Wanting what others have.

- Consumed by appearance or material things.
- Perfectionism.
- Allowing the inner critic to control your mind.

Humility

I started looking at my pride in my late twenties. In order to let go of my pride, I needed to replace it with something. I was told by a wise mentor to pray for humility. I began to research the word humility and here's what I found:

- Nonjudgmental.
- Someone who is selfless.
- Someone who surrenders their life to God.
- Someone who can apologize and take ownership.
- Being faithful and trusting; free from fear and worry.
- Someone who is gracious and practices gratitude.
- Someone who can walk away from an argument, especially when they believe they are right.
- Someone who can submit, when called to submit.
- Someone who is able to follow directions and rules.
- Appreciative of what they have.
- Able to praise and acknowledge other people's gifts and talents.
- Patient.
- Seeing oneself as equal to others; no less and no better than.
- Allowing yourself and others to make mistakes.
- Able to admit your limitations.

Ways to Practice Humility

We all struggle with ego and pride. Whether it comes out as arrogance toward others, self-pity, perfectionism, or low self-esteem, we all struggle with it. I didn't realize that allowing my inner critic to control my life was a form of pride. Once I truly learned what being prideful means, I became fully willing to make the necessary changes. The following are ways that I shifted my thinking from being prideful to being humble,

1. **Learn more about what it means to be prideful.** In order to shift my thinking from pride to humility, I had to first learn what being prideful looks like. I did this by googling the words ego and pride. I studied the meaning of pride by reading articles, short books and listening to audio podcasts. The more I learned, the more I became aware and determined to let go of my pride. The more I began to understand how my pride was affecting my relationship with myself, God and others, the more willing I became to change my thinking. The more I learned about pride, the more I realized that **I DO HAVE SOME CONTROL IN MY RELATIONSHIPS.** That control is in myself and how I view things.

2. **Learn about what it means to be humble.** Learning about pride made me willing to change. In order to change, I had to replace my old ways of thinking and behaving with new ones. I learned as much as I could about humility. I went through the same process, I googled humility and read articles, books and listened to podcasts during my long walks. Understanding humility helped me to put into words exactly what I was striving for. It gave me words to be able to express what I wanted and helped me to be able to have clear focus and set meaningful intentions.

3. **Spend more time with humble people.** Once I learned what it means to be humble, I began to identify the people in my life who had this quality. I made a point to spend more time with those people in my life so I could learn from them. I found that by spending more time with humble people, it became easier for me to practice humility. It became more normal for me to be humble.

4. **Pray and ask God for help and guidance.** As we know, change is hard. Letting go of my pride was a difficult task. And every now and then it creeps back up. I continue to pray for both awareness and willingness. Awareness allows me to see clearly what needs to be changed and willingness allows me to make the necessary changes. As long as I am willing to make the changes, God can transform and renew my thinking.

5. **Practice Grace and Forgiveness.** As we've learned in previous chapters, in order to fully let go of our anger, resentment, pride and ego, we must practice grace and forgiveness with both ourselves and others. We must be able to admit fault, take ownership, let go of perfectionism and expectations. We must be able to forgive. Being gracious and forgiving is being humble.

6. **Practice Gratitude.** Gratitude is another way of being humble. It is shifting a poor me attitude to an attitude of gratitude. It is shifting a negative perspective to a perspective of thankfulness. When we are thankful, we are not focused on ourselves or all of the things wrong with ourselves and others. When we are grateful, we are humble; we are less deserving and we are viewing our lives through spiritual eyes, rather human ones.

Challenges You May Face

Making the decision to let go of my pride with regard to my daughter's education wasn't an easy one. Honestly, it was out of complete desperation to feel peace in the situation that made me willing to seek a new way. I was bitter and angry and those feelings consumed me. In order to let go of my pride and adopt a humble attitude, I had to overcome some challenges. The following is a list of challenges you may experience when shifting from a prideful attitude to a humble attitude:

1. **You can expect to grieve expectations.** Pride comes from expectations we have over a person, place, thing or situation. Letting go of pride involves grieving our expectations. It is not an easy or comfortable process.

2. **It is a process and it takes time to learn humility and grieve our expectations.** Humility was not something that came natural for me. Humility meant letting go and grieving pride. Grieving is a process and takes time.

3. **You will have a battle in your head with the inner critic.** As you begin to acknowledge your pride, you can expect a visit from the inner critic. Your critic comes from your ego and pride. As you begin to make changes from pride to humility, your critic will become stronger and will challenge you creating a battle in your head. This battle can consume you, but only if you allow it to.

4. **You will make mistakes.** As you begin to recognize your pride, you will make changes to overcome it. You will make many mistakes, but rest assured that you will learn best from making those mistakes.

So Now What?

I spent most of my life living through ego and pride; either needing to be on top, or constantly pitying myself. It not only affected my ability to advocate for my children at school, but most importantly, it impacted my personal relationships, especially the one I had with myself. In order to surrender our pride and adopt a humble attitude, we must surrender our will and let go of we want or think should or should not happen. Letting go of pride releases the unnecessary pressures we take on and allows for a more peaceful flow in life. Take a moment to reflect on the forms of pride you may be taking on. Once you identify them, release them by asking the God of the universe for help. Practice self-compassion by allowing yourself to grieve and make mistakes as you rewire your thinking and make these significant changes in your life.

Questions for Reflection

Find a quiet space where there are little to no distractions. Take a moment in quiet to reflect on what you just read. When you are ready, answer the following questions in your journal.

1. What is your current understanding of pride? How has your understanding of pride changed after reading this chapter? Explain.

2. List the forms of pride you can relate to in your personal life. How does this pride affect your relationships with both yourself and others?

3. Does pride affect your life in any other ways? Please explain.

4. How can learning to practice humility change the way you view yourself and others? Explain.

5. Are you practicing humility in your life? Please give some examples and explain the effects of practicing humility. How might this situation have been different if you were prideful?

6. What steps can you take to begin to practice humility today?

Chapter 14

Gratitude

"You can always find the good in every situation, whether the situation be an opportunity for growth or a chance to do something different."

The final topic I will discuss is gratitude. Gratitude allows us to shift from a negative perspective to a perspective of thankfulness. Practicing gratitude does not minimize our hurts, but instead allows us to see the blessings that come from our hurts. It is the act of shifting our focus from the negative to the positive.

Throughout my journey of spiritual recovery, I learned that gratitude is one of the key components to shifting from old, unhealthy thought patterns, to positive, healthy patterns. Gratitude allows me to let go of what is going wrong and focus on what is going right. It allows me to let go of my expectations and be aware of the blessings in front of me. No matter how bad my circumstances are, I can always be grateful for something. Gratitude allows me to be humble and diminishes my pride and ego. Practicing gratitude allows me to see through spiritual eyes, rather human eyes. When I see through spiritual eyes, I find peace and balance.

One of the most difficult experiences I had in my life was losing the person I thought was my best friend. It was the most painful two years of my life. But some amazing things happened in those two years. As I began to practice gratitude, I became grateful for the process of grief. I also began to recognize why God was removing this person from my life. The relationship was toxic and harmful to my mental health. I was consumed by the relationship that I was not able to see the work I had in front of me; spiritual work that God was calling me to do and work that changed my life for the better. When this person abandoned our friendship, the grief consumed me and held me hostage to loneliness, depression, isolation, shame and guilt. Gratitude allowed me to be aware that I had a family right in front of me who loved me and wanted me. And because of that gratitude, I learned how to be present with my family because once that friend left, my wrapped in this relationship, I had abandoned all of my other relationships for this one. So, after she was gone, I had to start all over.

So many blessings came from the fallout of this friendship. I began to recognize unhealthy patterns of co-dependency in myself. I became aware that I had this subconscious need to be a hero in relationships; seeking to always fix and please. I began to recognize unhealthy patterns and personality traits in others that allowed me to work on setting healthy boundaries with people who only wanted to take from me or people who sought to push my buttons and create drama. I learned to recognize patterns in myself where I was the only person putting effort into relationships, being left to feel like I was annoying or burdening someone by wanting to spend time with them.

Gratitude allowed me to be grateful for this awareness. It allowed me to work on me and change things in me that then allowed me to hold space for healthier relationships. Gratitude allowed me to be thankful for my husband and children and see the true blessings they are in my life; blessings I see now that I took for granted. Gratitude allowed me to move from anger, guilt, shame and blame to being able to forgive those who have harmed me. And being able to forgive and accept the loss allowed me to heal and recover. Gratitude and acceptance allowed me to open new doors which led me to private practice, writing blogs and books, a new church family and healthier relationships with people in my life. And gratitude allows me to see these gifts instead of seeing the pain. Today I recognize my grief and know that it was a process I had to endure and embrace. But if I had to do it all over again, I would make the practice of gratitude a daily one from the start.

I have a client that I coach. A few years ago, she struggled with a divorce. Her ex-husband was cheating on her and she felt betrayed, alone and devastated. She suffered through grief and depression, mostly stuck in anger. During every session, I always ask my clients to list three things they are grateful for in their time of struggle; perhaps something that has come from the struggle. I usually get a raised eyebrow as if to say, "What do you mean grateful? This is the worst feeling and situation I've ever been through." But once this client began to think about the question, she was able to list more than three things. I sent her home that day asking her to make a gratitude list every day for the next month. She came back a month later with a completely different attitude and perspective and was in completely different spirits. Her anger had lifted and she could see her future filled with some hope. She was grateful for the pain she had endured and the loss she had suffered. She was able to understand that her devastating experience allowed her to see behaviors and things in herself that she could not see before; behaviors that kept her trapped in unhealthy relationships. She told me that practicing gratitude was one of the most important parts of her healing.

How to Live With an Attitude of Gratitude

Gratitude is a choice. We can choose to look at all the negative things around us or we can choose to find the gratitude in our situations. The following are the ways I was able to shift from grief to gratitude.

1. *Talk to someone who is able to help you shift your thinking from seeing the negative to being able to see the blessings in your pain or situation.*

2. *Keep a special journal or shoebox out where you can keep track of your daily blessings. List three things you are grateful for each day.*

3. *Pray to God, asking Him to reveal or help you see and recognize your blessings.*

4. *Surround yourself with people who live with an attitude of gratitude. This will help you to adopt this way of thinking. We are more likely to be like the people we surround ourselves with.*

5. *Download and listen to podcasts on the benefits of gratitude. Read articles, blogs or books about gratitude to reinforce this kind of thinking.*

6. *Read a daily gratitude devotional that will reinforce an attitude of gratitude.*

7. *Practice guided meditations that focus on gratitude.*

8. *Thank God for your blessings by naming them to Him.*

9. *Make the practice of gratitude a priority by setting aside time to do one of the above activities each day.*

10. *Volunteer at a shelter, hospital or atmosphere where there are people in need.*

Challenges You May Face

1. **Inner Critic.** The inner critic will try to steer you away from your attitude of gratitude by replaying the negative messages and stories in your mind.

2. **Time.** Again, our culture and the society that we live in is incredibly rushed and fast paced. In our minds we procrastinate and say that we will do it later or tomorrow. Putting it off will only make the practice harder to incorporate into your daily life. Start today.

So Now What?

Take the time to be aware of the blessings in your life. By adopting an attitude of gratitude, you will begin to shift from living through the inner critic to living through your inner coach. There are always things to be grateful for. Each and every day you wake up is a blessing. Having eyes that see color and beauty in nature and ears that hear the sounds around us is a blessing. Having legs to walk with and hands to hold with is a blessing. Having the people in our lives that we do have are a blessing. Life is a gift that can be erased in a blink of an eye. You don't want to spend your life looking through eyes of negativity or unappreciation; only seeing the hurt, pain and struggle. There is so much more in life. Don't take for granted the gifts in front of you. No matter how bad a situation is, there is always something good happening in it. God is good and He will provide, especially during the darkest times. If you struggle to recognize gratitude, pray and ask God to show you and help you to see what you cannot yet see.

Questions for Reflection

Find a quiet space where there are little to no distractions. Take a moment in quiet to reflect on what you just read. When you are ready, answer the following questions in your journal.

1. What are some of the struggles you are currently facing? List the positive things that are happening during these struggles or as a result of these struggles.

2. What are some of the ways you currently practice gratitude?

3. What ideas in this chapter can you implement into your life that will allow you to adopt an attitude of gratitude?

4. What kinds of things might your inner critic say as a result of practicing gratitude?

5. How can you reassure the inner critic that it is wrong?

6. Do you need to set aside time each day for gratitude? If so, then how and what will you do to ensure you have time to do this?

7. List 5 things you are especially grateful for today.

Chapter 15

Breaking the Cycle in Your Home

"Teach through action, not through mouth. They can't hear what you are saying, but they can see what you are doing."

Guess what! You made it through this book! I am so proud of you for taking the time, energy, and effort it takes to push through these chapters. The topics we discussed in this guide are not easy. What you learned in this guide uncovers truth, removes denial and deters resistance. I am hoping that you have experienced growth by working through this.

This chapter is called "Breaking the Cycle in Your Home." This is because that is exactly what you are doing by working through this book. You are renewing your mind, body and soul and making changes in your life that will not only impact you, but will impact all those around you. By learning how to deal with stress by living intuitively, you are breaking free from toxic behaviors and toxic relationships and hopefully improving your self-esteem, confidence and mood. You are becoming a model of hope and truth for others, especially the people in your own home. It doesn't matter if you are sixteen or sixty, you are changing the world one person at a time.

Modeling this truth for others is the most powerful way to change old, destructive, negative patterns. Think back to our very first chapter on stress. Stress triggers the fight or flight response. Stress is triggered by change. You are changing. Therefore, at times, you may be the cause of stress to those around you. By modeling these principles within yourself, you break down walls and defense mechanisms in others. Instead of people responding with fear, they begin to question what we are doing different that is making such a profound impact in your life. And eventually they begin to ask questions and explore self-renewal on their own.

Prescription for Self-Renewal

In order to fully recover from stress, we must connect to our intuition and make time to practice self-care. But as we've discussed in this book, reducing stress is not just about intuition and self-care. There are many important steps and changes we need to make in ourselves in order to rewire our old ways of thinking and doing. Our societal, cultural, family and religious traditions and beliefs have a tremendous impact on the expectations we have of ourselves and others. In order to let go of those expectations, we must grieve them through self-compassion and acceptance. The following is a recap of all the important things we need to do in order to renew our mind, body and soul and live a life of intuitive living and intention. I call it my prescription for healthy and balanced living.

1. *Share your story.*
2. *Learn to recognize your stress.*
3. *Connect with your intuition.*
4. *Incorporate daily self-care to manage stress and stay connected to your intuition.*
5. *Let go of expectations of yourself and others.*
6. *Access your inner coach.*
7. *Embrace acceptance through self-compassion.*
8. *Set healthy boundaries with those around you.*
9. *Ask for help and surround yourself with people who reflect positive self-care and energy.*
10. *Surrender to the God of your understanding.*
11. *Practice prayer, meditation and yoga.*
12. *Forgive others and allow yourself to be forgiven.*

13. Live with intention.

14. Be humble.

15. Practice daily gratitude.

16. Break the cycle in your home by modeling the Mind, Body, Spirit Approach to Self-Renewal.

17. Share your testimony with others.

Ways to "Break the Cycle" in Your Home

When you make the decision to change your thinking, your ways and your life, you will naturally have an effect on others. By making positive changes in your life, you create new rules and expectations in the world around you; healthier ones. The following are ways to break old patterns of self-destructive thinking and behaviors in your home, community and world around you.

1. **Model self-care and intuitive living to others.** Our children learn to love themselves by watching us love ourselves. If we hate ourselves, our children learn to hate themselves. If we are not good enough to ourselves, they internalize that they too are not good enough. If we judge ourselves, our children learn to do the same. And let's face it, we are our own worst critics and enemies. Model intuitive living and practice self-care. Talk aloud when you've notice that you've made a mistake and you no longer feel so good. Share your success with them, the practices that are having a positive impact on you.

2. **Listen to those around you with intention.** Sometimes we talk too much instead of just taking the time to listen. Listening allows the other person to process and explore their own thoughts, feelings and behaviors. Listen without judgement. Allow the other person to have their own feelings and experiences.

3. **Let go of your expectations of those around you.**
   Expectations lead to grief. We all know that feeling grief is
   not fun. Practice living without expectations. Living this
   way brings about a sense of freedom and peace.

4. **Accept the boundaries of others.** Don't internalize or take
   things so personally. You are practicing setting healthy
   boundaries, so allow others to set them with you.

5. **Forgive and be forgiven.** Giving and receiving grace are
   two of the most precious gifts we have. It allows us to let
   go of our faults, failures and mistakes as well as the faults,
   failures and mistakes of others. Being able to let go of hurts
   and accept forgiveness are two of the hardest things to do.
   Modeling this for others demonstrates the act of grace and
   creates a more peaceful environment free of shame and
   guilt. It allows us to live with intention and purpose.

6. **Recognize humility in others.** Have you ever heard the
   saying that praise works better than punishment? Point out
   the humility in others, rather than focusing on the pride and
   ego. Doing this reinforces humility and communicates that
   it was a more effective response or reaction.

7. **Pray for the ones in your home, community and the world
   around you.** Prayer is one of the most powerful tools we
   have. Use it. Pray for the people around you, whether you
   like them or not. Prayer works and it fosters change.

8. **Say thank you.** Saying "thank you" reinforces and
   communicates that you appreciate what another person did
   or did not do. It builds on the positive things in a
   relationship, rather on the things that are not right.

9. **Be persistent and don't give up.** You can expect to take two steps forward and one step back. The biggest thing I learned on this healing journey is that it is never-ending. We are always changing and growing. So when you find yourself taking one step backward, be persistent and don't stop trying. You will always find that you take two steps forward.

10. **Be patient with the process of change.** As we've discussed many times, change takes time. It is a process and it can be an ugly process. Patience allows for change to happen.

Challenges You May Face

One of the truths I learned before writing this book is to "just be". I was so excited when I learned all of the things in this book that I am now teaching you. I wanted to tell everyone and I wanted to tell them every minute of the day. I was obsessed with helping people to see what I could see. I felt like I had the answers to life and was doing a disservice by not sharing. But I quickly learned that people are not always ready to hear what I have to say. The following are the challenges I have faced from others while practicing the RENEWED approach to living:

1. **Resistance and denial from others.**
2. **Anger from others.**
3. **Shame, guilt and blame from others.**
4. **Depression in others.**

Do you recognize a pattern here? The pattern is grief. That's right! When you change your ways of thinking and being, you trigger change in others. It's called the *Systems Theory*. It can affect not just family members, but friends, co-workers and sometimes even acquaintances too. You see, the people around you are used to you being a certain way. This includes behaving, responding and reacting a certain way to them. When you begin to change those ways, they have a choice to either resist those changes or embrace them. Remember, in order to embrace them, they need to grieve them. I found this to be extremely enlightening. Understanding the grief that others will encounter as a result of my changes, helped me to be more compassionate, patient and understanding and much less angry and defensive. Remember, the last stage of grief is acceptance. So, when you are receiving the negative effects of someone's grief, you will be able to gauge where they are in their journey of acceptance with you. You will be able to better understand with compassion and patience and know that acceptance is lurking around the corner of their grief.

So Now What?

The great thing about this guide is that it is something you can refer back to anytime you feel ungrounded. So don't just stop here. Come back to this guide again and work through it. Or better yet, become a RENEWED Certified Life Coach and teach it to others. Gather a few people who are looking for renewal and continue this journey together. Model intuitive living and make time for self-care. By modeling this approach to those around you, you will not only help others, but you will also build a healthier support system with those around you.

If you feel called to share this program with others by becoming a RENEWED Certified Program Coach, please visit my website at www.**renewedmindbodyspirit.wordpress.com**.

Questions for Reflection

Find a quiet space where there are little to no distractions. Take a moment in quiet to reflect on what you just read. When you are ready, answer the following questions in your journal.

1. Have you begun to see changes in your home as a result of practicing Intuitive Living and the "Mind, Body, Approach to Self-Renewal"? Please describe.

2. Take a moment to reflect on the most important lessons you gained from this book. Write your own "Prescription for Living". You can use my list or write your own.

3. How can you model these truths to those around you and break the cycle in your home or environment?

4. What are some challenges you have faced along the way while working through this book?

5. Can you apply a *Systems Theory* or the *Stages of Grief* to help you understand these challenges? Please explain.

6. What can you do today to follow your "Prescription for Living" and begin breaking the cycle in your home or environment?

Epilogue

My Testimony

Thank you so much for allowing me the time and space to share my journey and experiences with you. You've now been able to read through all of the important lessons I learned throughout my spiritual journey of growth. I want to take a moment to share with you the outcome I've experienced as a result of following the RENEWED approach to intuitive living.

I started this book with my story to explain where I came from and what my cultural, societal, family and religious background was like growing up. Like most of you who chose to read this book, I grew up not knowing how to take care of my whole self. My inability to live intuitively was the result of the culture and society we live in. That society and culture impacted my grandparents, who projected what they learned onto my parents, who projected what they learned onto me. I had to re-learn how to listen to my inner wisdom and inner self. I had to learn to connect to my intuition. And most importantly, I had to learn how to manage my stress by practicing self-care so that I could stay connected to true self.

So much has changed as a result of relearning how to listen to my mind, body and spirit. The biggest thing I learned was how to have faith in God. During my mini breakdown, when I decided to finally learn how to cope with stress, I was challenged to trust in God. I chose to believe in Him and chose to ask Him for help. As I stated in the beginning of this book, I've always believed in God, but I had never truly surrendered my life to Him.

My relationship with God started with a physical and mental problem. I was desperate to feel better; desperate for my anxiety to go away. I was desperate for sleep. I was desperate for peace. I had little energy, but tons of motivation to get well.

Since turning my life over to God and learning how to listen to my intuition so many things have changed. I learned how to accept that life is a process. I may pray for something to be restored or healed, but most of the time, it doesn't happen overnight. It takes time. I learned how to be grateful for my troubles. I learned how to view my troubles as a chance to learn and grow. I wouldn't say that I get excited when I have troubles, but I do have peace during my troubles.

Today I can recognize my stress within a matter of hours to a few days. I no longer spend week after week in stress. Today I know that when I start to feel uneasy, then I need to take a step back and assess my path. I still encounter stress and I still encounter depression, but I know that it will pass. I also know that it can be a sign that something in my life is off or needs to change.

When I started to live intuitively, my fears of people and fears of talking went away. I am now writing, blogging and beginning to speak to groups of people. I am leading groups and teaching. These are things I never would have imagined myself doing as they used to cause me a great deal of anxiety. And best of all, today the inner critic does not bother me after I talk in a social setting. I no longer obsess about what I said or didn't say or about what they think of me. Intuitive living allows me to live for God, therefore, I do not need to be afraid. If God brings me to it, then He will provide the resources I need to get through it.

I learned how to accept my faults and failures and know today that I am not perfect, nor am I expected to be. I know that it is okay to mess up and I do it a lot and am able to smile during and after my mistakes. Today I know how to laugh; I know how to have a sense of humor.

I also know how to grieve. I know how to recognize expectations and I know how to feel the loss and rejection that comes when my expectations are not met. I no longer run or hide from my problems, nor do I need to get defensive.

I no longer struggle with bulimia. I am learning to fully embrace my body for what it is today. I am intentional each day with physical self-care and I do the best that I can. I continue to struggle with emotional eating at times, but I think everyone does. I am able to remind myself that I am not perfect, so I am not going to eat perfect every day. I am much gentler with myself. I do not restrict food today. I enjoy food to the full. I love food and I love the different seasons in nature and holidays that are included. I enjoy every bit of eating, especially during the fall and winter seasons.

Today I engage in exercise that I enjoy. I love to cycle with my husband, walk my dogs, lift weights and jog on occasion while catching up on my favorite television shows. I do not put the pressure I used to put on myself to overwork my body. I love the movement I do and enjoy my time at the gym, on the bike or in nature with my dogs.

Today I have purpose. I understand that I am here on this earth for a reason. I seek that purpose every day. I understand that it changes and evolves over time. I own my own practice and am building programs that teach people how to take care of themselves. This is one of my favorite changes I've encountered. I feel like a butterfly who exploded out of its cocoon. I love my job and feel so blessed to be doing it. Work brings me a sense of fulfillment and validation. And when I take on too much (which I can do sometimes), I take a step back and regroup by adjusting my schedule.

Today I have friends. I have real friends who care about me. I have friends and family that I know would be there for me if I needed it. But more importantly, I am not dependent on them for happiness nor do I need them to feel good about myself. I have healthy, loving relationships.

I have a church that I absolutely love. I cannot imagine my life without this church. One of the best things I ever took the risk to do was to explore my faith. Today I not only attend church, but I volunteer at my church. I lead at my church. Most importantly, I grow at my church. I am not afraid at my church. I do not feel bad at my church. I have no guilt or shame at my church.

Throughout this journey, God has become the most important part of my life. I used to put my faith in money, relationships and food. But today I know God. Knowing God allows me to live without fear as well as to have freedom from guilt and shame.

My journey has been long and it has been hard. But I would not change one part of my journey. Today I like myself a lot. I am a pretty cool person who does pretty cool things. I could not say that before. My journey has taught me how to let go of some of the hardest things I've ever been challenged to let go of. I know I still have a long journey ahead filled with continuous healing and growth, but I have faith and fully believe that I will continue that journey. My life gets better and better and the blessings get bigger and bigger.

There are circumstances and situations I dread in the future to come, mostly having to do with losses of loved ones, because let's face it, that is never easy. But I know that I have God and I also know that this life is not eternal. I know that I do have an eternal, spiritual life waiting for me when I am done here. This gives me great peace.

RENEWED is a program I've developed as a result of my personal and professional experience in working with people who struggle with stress, anxiety, depression, relationships and even addictions. My hope is that it will reach people and help them too. I believe that God has a plan for this program. I believe that He used me to create this to help others. While I have hopes for what will become of this, I know that no matter what happens, God is in control.

I thank you again for allowing me to share my journey. I thank you for sharing yours. I hope you will take some time to reflect on what you've read in this book and most importantly, I hope you will take time to pray and ask God what it is He wants you to see and do with this.

To end this journey, please take some time to reflect on what you've learned and what has changed since you began this book. Write your testimony!

Peace and blessings,
Katie

A Word of Thanks

Thank you for taking the time to read this book. The ideas and opinions expressed are based off my years of professional and personal experience. They may be somewhat different from what you are used to, but they are how I've been able to change my old ways of thinking and heal my anxiety, depression, co-dependency and eating disorder. I am currently using this guide as a life coaching tool. I offer a 17 week Online Personal Life Coaching Program or 17 Week Group Programs. I also offer a Certification Program if you would like to facilitate RENEWED groups in your area. For more details you can check out my website at
www.renewedmindbodyspirit.wordpress.com.

Peace and blessings,
Katie LaPlant, MSW, LICSW

www.renewedmindbodyspirit.wordpress.com

Made in the USA
Middletown, DE
10 January 2017